1989
A NOVELLA

By
Kirven Tillis

1989: A Novella

First Printing: 2025

ISBN: 978-1-967464-05-0

Ordering Information:
Special discounts are available on quantity purchases by corporations, associations, educators, and others. For details, contact the publisher at the email listed below.

U.S. trade bookstores and wholesalers:

Please contact
kickinoutmedia@gmail.com

1989: A Novella

DEDICATION

To adolescence and all the unforgettable turbulence of becoming an adult.

This book is dedicated to LL, Macka, and Todd

1989: A Novella

TABLE OF CONTENTS

1989: A Novella

May

"Fuck all y'all"

The final bell rang. School was out for the summer.

LL jumped from his seat, pulled out a few eggs from his pocket and side armed them like he was skipping rocks across the canal at the end of Allen Lane.

There were critical differences.

There was no lake, only a ceiling. In a high school cafeteria, with an assistant principal watching over us, the eggs didn't skip, they splattered off of the ceiling tiles and as the shells and their innards rained over the students and others in the cafeteria all hell broke loose.

LL was a slim kid, a charmer. While he was quick to laugh and smile during the fun times, he took no shit off anybody.

I can only chalk it up to mischief when it came to him throwing the eggs.

I don't know of an incident before or since that sent Ross S. Sterling High School into such an uproar.

Kids started screaming and throwing papers in the air.

We immediately ran toward the bus ramp. The school commons had random melees breaking out. A boy fell down and kids started kicking and stomping on him. Two girls were engaged in mortal combat, as both of them were

1989: A Novella

locked together by the hair that was firmly clenched in each other's hands. They were spinning like some sort of bizarro carnival ride. Kids were running and screaming. The scene was pure chaos; I had to throw a couple of kids out of the way as we ran to bus 19.

I was wanting to tell LL something but he was nowhere to be seen. He totally vanished into the belly of the riot. Out of the corner of my eye, I saw something. It was a bookbag that was headed straight toward me. Deflecting it with my Trapper Keeper, I slapped the boy upside the head.

Once I stepped outside, it was a different world. Kids were boarding the buses like normal. I went to the second column of buses; that's where I saw number 19. My eyes met the bus driver's eyes. Miss Yolanda had a look that knew that she was in for a long afternoon. I went to my normal spot in the back of the bus and waited for LL to board. All the other kids were loading up. I saw all my friends, Corey, Plick, and Dorian, coming to the back. Evelyn, Dawn, and Tashia boarded, laughing, they were talking shit like always. Finally, as the bus is getting ready to file out behind all the others, LL shows up, with the neck of his shirt stretched; his face had a smirk that said he'd been kicking somebody's ass and got the best of them.

Bus 19 was something else. As we were getting ready to leave, Troy pulled out a spray canister of mace. When the bus lurches forward, he takes the canister and points it at the bus next to us preparing to spray it in their windows.

Don't do it, I thought. The bus is moving, I thought.

1989: A Novella

I had to speak up…

"Yo, don't spray that shit! The bus is about to…"

I couldn't get the words out in time. Troy sprayed the mace and it blew back into all the people behind him, including myself.

There was a chorus of sneezing, laughing, coughing, and gagging.

Miss Yolanda just looked and smirked as she sped over the speed bumps to give us a bit of jolt to add insult to injury. She hated us. She had every right to.

This was a bus that citizens would force to pull over because people would flick pennies out of the windows and hit cars. This was a bus where kids would yell and scream throughout the entire bus trip to and from school. The only exception was on the occasional cold winter morning when it was too cold and too early to be disruptive.

The afternoons were never quiet and the ride home on the last day of school was certainly no exception. After the air on the bus was cleared of the pungent, stinging smells of mace, all of the kids on the bus began to talk and laugh about any and everything.

There was excitement in the air. It was a distinct feeling of anticipation of Summer and all that goes with it. As I sat and talked with LL and the rest of the crew, I thought about how exciting it was to have one more year of school left.

1989: A Novella

This one was going to be different, a few of my closest friends were seniors. They were about to graduate in a few hours and hit the real world. They were going to college and to the military. A couple were going to work.

I couldn't wait for them to walk the stage and become high school graduates. These were my boys. They taught me the ropes and set the stage for the best high school experience that a kid could have. I was a year younger and they let me roll. They took me under their collective wing and I embraced it all.

We were the FTP, the Flat Top Posse, a collective of kids who ran track and loved hip-hop. We ran, we danced, we rapped. We went to parties and took them over. There was no, "Do the ladies run this mutha…" and there was no, "Do the fellas run this mutha…" because chants of "FTP! FTP!" would overrule the dance floor and my crew and those with us would have the best time.

Obviously, with a name like FTP, one would think that all of us would have a flat top of some sort. That was mostly true, except for one member named Macka. He was called Macka because he behaved like the man that the Fresh Prince said was first out of the limousine. Small in stature yet freakishly strong and athletic, Macka looked every bit of the enforcer when we went out, when we snuck into clubs. He just had that look. Once, we went to San Jacinto Mall to hang out and talk to the girls. We hung out in The Market and played video games at Yesterdays. Afterwards we went across Garth Road to McDonalds to get something to eat. We had decided that Macka would hold all our money and pay for everything. We strolled into

1989: A Novella

McDonald's and ordered. Then, after everyone had ordered their food, I turned toward my best friend and said for all to hear:

"Macka, pay the lady!"

The FTP parts like the Red Sea and Macka, with his hat slammed down on his head like Chuck D, pulled out the bankroll and paid for all the food. The people around us were in a mishmash of shock and astonishment as we waited on our orders to come up. We turned the fast food joint into a party until we left. This was the norm any and every time we were at a party or public space. It was going to be a good time, no matter what!

This was my life and I was enjoying every minute of it.

1989: A Novella

June

Summer began and I got a part-time job working retail at San Jacinto Mall. Miller's Outpost was a retail store that specializes in men's and women's casual wear. I spent anywhere from 15 to 20 hours a week there finger spacing shirts and keeping the jeans wall looking tidy and neat. I loved my job and as a result of working there, I knew virtually every sales person from Chess King, down past The Gap and JeansWest. From there the floor would slope down to a major intersection that led to anchor stores, JC Penny and Mervyn's. Typically, I would continue my journey down past the intersection, stopping to look at the latest kicks in Foot Locker before proceeding down to the Market where all the food establishments, the movie theater, and the game room were located.

I loved being at the mall. The mall rat who actually held down a job. San Jacinto was the greatest place on earth where people from all over Texas and other states would come to shop. When I was at work, my friends would come to see me and my manager would get irritated at the traffic that I would bring in because they were broke and not spending much money. She seemed to ignore that the residual effect was that other people came in and spent money because of the kids being in the store.

I would be in the store providing entertainment on slow nights. We'd laugh and talk until our "rivals" across the hall at Chess King would want to come by to see what we were doing that caused so much commotion.

"You are so silly!"

1989: A Novella

Connie, the assistant manager, would always tell me this while she would laugh until her face would turn beet red and tears would well up in her eyes.

Liz, who was the store manager, would just look and shake her head.

"What are we going to do with you?"

I always suggested a raise. Laughter would ensue.

Someone had to show them the latest dances. Someone had to imitate the characters from classic cartoons. Someone.

Me. I was that someone.

One night we were cleaning up and I found a rather large pair of tights. I took the tights and went into one of the dressing rooms to put them on. The dressing rooms were like old western saloons with the swinging doors. I called my co-workers to the dressing room area and told them that I needed to show them something.

They all knew that I was up to my usual shenanigans, but they had no clue what I had in store.

With a hearty push, I flung the door open and stepped into the doorway. With the tights on. With my shirt tucked in.

I placed my hands on each side of the door jamb and began gyrating sensually.

1989: A Novella

I was grinding.

Pelvic thrusting.

Dancing sensually.

I turned toward the door jamb and bent one of my legs at the knee as I danced provocatively while moving that leg up and down on the door jamb. My managers plus my co-workers, Greg and Nisha, lost it. They were laughing so hard; it was difficult for me to stay in character. I eventually made my way out on the floor, humping and pelvic thrusting my way into a comedic frenzy where we were all laughing so hard that tears were flowing and stomachs were hurting.

The job was easy for me. Customer service was right up my alley as a person who got through school being a class clown and a friend to all.

There was only one problem for me and the job that I loved so much. I didn't have a car, and many times I had to bum a ride to work. Usually, my mama would take me or Macka would. Fortunately, I was able to make some money to have a few things and be able to hang out with my friends. I never knew how important it was to have people who could take you to and from work. I never knew…

June was in full swing. Heat and humidity were the norms. The dog days of summer were just that. When I wasn't working, I'd hang out with Macka and LL. We'd spend the heat of the day playing video games. We'd play football or

1989: A Novella

basketball in the evenings. AJ, Rod, James, Wade and other members of the crew would come by and hang out.

One day we were all hanging and the graduates were talking about their future plans.

AJ was a ladies' man who bore a strong resemblance to Play of the rap group Kid N Play. A shade under 6ft tall, he was lean and athletic. He lived with his aunt and uncle and was very much spoiled by hood standards. Don't get me wrong, he wasn't a brat, he was just fortunate.

We had known each other forever because our uncles were a part of a group of men who were skilled craftsmen. They wore coveralls on the daily. Long sleeved. Short sleeved. To work. To church. Loungewear…It was the daily fit with a nice pair of loafers. They kept a carpenter's pencil behind one ear because the urge could hit and all of a sudden, they are building a cabinet or planning an addition to a home. We met during these sessions as two kids who were just trying to play and hang out. As we got older track and field, the love of motorcycles, and music bonded us.

As a sophomore he had a brown Mustang. He installed a system and we'd go wherever we could, whenever we could.

When he came over, the Juneteenth Parade was the topic. This was always a contentious subject for the both of us because of an incident that happened at the end of the parade when we were younger…

1989: A Novella

The Juneteenth Celebration and Parade was the biggest event of the Summer. The parade began on Jones Road in the section of McNair known as "French Town" due to the high concentration of Creoles from southwestern Louisiana that migrated and settled into that area of town.

From Jones Road, the parade headed south to Harrison, passing Johnson and Frazier Funeral Home, Mr. Page's liquor store, and his washateria. It continued to Harrison and Broad, where we turned east, rolling past Harlem Street, the elementary school, and over the

railroad tracks. From there, the parade went south on Wade Road toward I-10, looped up the feeder, and entered King's Colony. After a brief pass-through, it exited back onto the feeder and returned to Wade Road, heading toward McNair.

That's when things got dicey. Everyone continued past Broad and up Wade Road to "The Park."

The Park—a big rec center and green space—was named after local legends JD Walker and Edna Mae Washington. Folks from the area would say they were headed to JD Walker or just The Park.

The argument was inevitable.

"You can ride with me Kirv.", AJ said with a mischievous smirk.

He was setting me up.

Oblivious to what was about to happen, I looked up.

1989: A Novella

"Yeah mayne, we can represent in the 'Stang"

I was cool riding with my boy in his car in the parade because it was a chance for me to hang with my dude as he was headed to Ft. McClellan in a matter of weeks.

AJ seized the opportunity to pounce.

"At least you won't be running into me this year."

I couldn't believe this dude set me up.

"There you go, you ran into me!", was my counter.

"You ran into me!" was his quick reply.

I'm about to lose it.

"How you gonna say that when I was at the park and already turned around?"

Macka, Bam Bam and Mario sat amused. Laughing. Waiting for the inevitable...

I stood up, "Nigga! You ran into me! Yo' ass always trying to say somebody ran into you when you ran into me!"

Macka, Bam Bam, and Mario are still laughing.

When we were kids, there would be a moment when the parade was over, the fire truck would turn to go back into the neighborhood, all of the go karts, mini bikes, and bicycles would haul ass to The Park. One year, AJ and I

12

drove go karts. He had a black one-seater, almost like a dune buggy. I had a red two-seater. The clutch was modified so that I could drive faster than the kart was intended to go.

The reality is that two go karts were headed toward one another. When one driver, that would be me, went in one direction, the other driver, also known as AJ, would make the same yet opposite maneuver. This happened three consecutive times until we hit each other head on.

We argued about it from that moment forward.

"Check this out, Check this out!" This was AJ's favorite phrase, especially when he was trying to make a point.

Macka, Bam Bam, and Mario tried to stifle their laughs to hear what he was going to say.

"If you just would have went in the opposite direction when I did, we wouldn't have wrecked!"

Macka, Bam Bam, and Mario looked at me.

I looked at them.

I looked back at AJ.

"Everytime I would turn, yo dumbass would turn in the same way, check your glasses Mr. Magoo!"

We all started laughing and got back to the topic at hand.

1989: A Novella

Juneteenth was serious business. Girls from all over would be there. McNair. Baytown. Barrett. LaPorte. Even Houston and Louisiana girls would make their way to The Park and hang out for the day listening to music and checking out all the food and craft vendors there.

We were going to get our mack on and meet some girls.

There was only one girl's phone number that I wanted to get. Nell was her name and I was smitten. I thought she was beautiful. She had pretty brown skin, burnt sienna to be exact, and she wore braces. It was something about girls in braces that I found attractive. Plus, she would wear her hair in an asymmetrical bob with the curls on top like Salt N Pepa; I had to get that number.

She went to Lee High School, our crosstown rival. I was cool with her brother, Gerald, who I got to know through running track. I knew she was going to be showing up sooner or later so I just spent the majority of the day hanging out with Wade, Mario, Macka, and AJ. We were kicking it throughout the day, eating and having fun.

"Yo, did you see them girls from LaPorte?" Mario said as he looked at three girls who were walking across the parking lot toward DJ Suga Bear's set up. Macka and Mario were checking out some girls in biker shorts who were walking around trying to be seen as they approached the area where the DJ was set up.

"That's ole girl."

"Which one KO?"

14

1989: A Novella

"The one on the left in the bright green"

"What ole girl?"

AJ was confused as Mario and Macka were deciding to go and holla at them to see what was up.

"Come on mayne, You remember ole girl!"

"From where?"

"From that Party in LP! Remember you was dancing with her?"

One night we were at a party in La Porte. The DJ played "Tonight" by Ready for the World and as AJ was dancing with her, I happened to look his way. AJ had a handful of the girl's ass in his hand and he was slightly bent over with his right leg cocked and balanced by a tip toe. He started humping ole girl like he was a dog in heat. I never let him live it down.

"Dancing when?"

I immediately assumed the awkward position and started humping the air like a mangy German Shepherd trying to get it for the last time.

Mack and Mario were cackling. AJ gave me a playful shove and I almost fell over because it's hard to keep your balance with one leg cocked, on a tip toe.

I busted out laughing. AJ did too.

1989: A Novella

"Oh yeah!"

"OLE GIRL!" was said in unison by the 4 of us.

AJ said her name was Kathryn and she was pretty. Light brown with wavy silky hair, she was a stunner. AJ went over to reacquaint himself and Macka and Mario joined him to try and meet her friends.

I had other ideas.

I saw my other friends from school over by the community center. I walked over there to see what was up.

I saw my friends Wade and Adrian. we dapped and I asked them what was going on.

"Sup Dawg?" Adrian looked at me smiling.

"You know!"

We all started laughing as that brief exchange meant that we were doing well and trying to find a girl to talk to.

As fate would have it, we were in a spot that became crowded rather quickly.

Wade and I had the highest flattops in the area. We were like brothers, not only because we were similarly built, but we had the uncanny ability to say the same things and the most random times. Quotes. Song lyrics. Catchphrases. It was totally wild how we would say the same things and practically die laughing every time it happened. Combine

16

that with the ability to dance and talk plenty of shit, we had a tendency to draw a crowd.

Adrian would just lay low and smile, He was the shy brother who wasn't shy at all. An incredible athlete, Adrian was about that action and not really about talking until he met the object of his affection and she was usually one of the prettiest girls wherever we were. He'd laugh at us and Wade and I were the only ones who really got him talking and acting up. If we went somewhere and he danced, It was really going to be a good time to be had by all!

We would basically become The Three Musketeers. Three dudes who thought alike and always were hanging together.

We met in 6th grade. I was the only kid from McNair at Baytown Junior. Wade and I actually met in Pre-K at Miss Caroline's and I met Adrian at a 5th grade playday at Roseland Park when we were the best athletes on the playground from Harlem and San Jacinto elementaries, respectively. We were best friends who became closer when we all ended up going to Sterling High together.

Sounds of music echoed through the park. More and more people came to gather near the community center where Wade, Adrian and myself would be eventually joined by the majority of the FTP. We were all talking, laughing and hanging out. Before long the sun was starting to set and the parking lot became illuminated by the various light poles that surrounded the parking lot.

1989: A Novella

Eventually, Suga Bear played the music that started what everyone was waiting for, the dancing.

Rod started popping and moving around via various renditions of the moonwalk. We were all surrounding him, moving and grooving to the beats that Suga Bear had blaring out of the speakers. Todd and AJ were next and started doing some moves in tandem including the Patty Duke, and the Steve Martin.

A good time was being had by all.

I knew this would be a good time to impress Nell, so Wade and I made our way into the circle. Everyone knew that we were about to go off. We approached the middle of the circle, squaring up like we were about to fight each other. Suddenly, while face to face, we simultaneously lifted our right legs and leaned forward. Wade grabbed my right leg at the ankle and I grabbed his. We both hopped clockwise and when we made the 360-degree rotation we released legs.

It was at this time that we would do our rendition of the kick step. Everyone loved our version as we kicked feet and backed off a couple of times we'd resume and added a half turn as if we were going to move away from each other only to turn back and do more kick stepping. We would conclude by doing a double kick and going back in to grab arms to do another 360 while our right feet touched in the kicking position.

Everyone went crazy but we weren't done.

1989: A Novella

The entire FTP came together and Macka assumed a hardcore stance in the middle of us and on cue we all started doing "The Macka".

"The Macka" was like The Peanuts on steroids. Everyone would jump up and down, criss-crossing legs right over left and left over right with each exuberant impact. Our arms would be pushed down with one arm coming in front while the other one would be in the back, alternating with each jump. This was repeated about 5-7 times and then everyone would start dapping and yelling FTP until we decided to stop for the moment. It was the dance derived from the legendary running man that we credited Macka with creating.

As everyone was settling down. I approached Nell.

"Sup girl?"

"Hey."

"How's your summer so far?"

"It's alright."

"Cool. Where your brother at?"

"I think he with Greg 'nem."

"What you doin' tonight?"

"Nothing really, we hadn't really talked about going anywhere...Y'all?"

1989: A Novella

"We probably just gonna go back and hang out on the Lane."

"The Lane?"

"The coldest street around here, Allen Lane"

"Boy Please!"

"Girl Please!"

Nell laughed. I knew at this point that I needed to make my move because I had her laughing.

"So you gonna give me your number so I can call you?"

"Why would I want to do that?"

I smirked. She smiled.

"Because you need to get some of this aspectness."

"Ass what?"

I smiled. She smirked.

"This aspectness girl? So you can see the aspect of me being your man."

We smiled.

Nell gave me her number…

1989: A Novella

After I got the number, it was time to move on and see what could be seen and do what could be done.

I made my way back to the fellas and they all gave me the business because they saw Nell give me her number. It didn't matter because I was on cloud 9.

Later that evening things started to wind down and we left the park and went back to The Lane where we hung out, sang songs, and talked about girls until the wee hours of the morning.

Eventually, it was just Mario, Macka, and I, singing "Chance for Our Love" and "Always and Forever". We'd sit under the carport at my house talking about girls, teasing Mario for being scared of our neighbor Courtney. Macka was just totally captivated by this girl named Tutti. They were friends; he never really could get the nerve to see if it could go further.

"Dawg you trippin. You need to be trying to get up on that."

Macka stared at me as Mario gave me some dap and said, "Hell yeah, she fine mayne, what you waiting on?"

Macka looked at the both of us. We could see the look of unrequited love in his face.

"We're just friends."

Mario sat up a little bit taller.

1989: A Novella

"You need to let her know how you feel, that could be your gal!"

I dapped Mario and we started talking "aspectness" and how she needed to get some "aspect" from Macka.

He looked at us like the clowns that we were.

We all laughed and then the tone got a little somber.

Macka looked up and as his smile evaporated, he told us that his parents were thinking about moving.

"I don't want to move."

We were stunned because none of us moved off the Lane since we were kids. Allen Lane was where it was at. It was friendship. It was love. This was the street that bonded us for life, we were not supposed to separate because our parents were moving away.

"What about your brothers, can't you just live there with them?"

Macka did not respond.

Soon it was time to go inside. After freshening up, I called Nell.

"Hello?"

Her voice, soft and sweet, made me a little nervous.

1989: A Novella

"Hello, May I speak to Nell please?"

"Hey, This is Kirven."

"Hey."

"What's up?"

"Not Much, I'm just chillin' in my room."

"Me too."

"My Daddy said he knows your Daddy."

"He grew up in Oak Addition."

"Yeah, that's what my Daddy said...Hey can I call you back?"

"Yeah, call me back."

"Okay. Bye."

"Bye."

In the days to come I talked to Nell a few more times. We had no chemistry. Conversations were all duds. We eventually just stopped talking.

As June came to an end, the summer heat was just beginning. We'd play video games in the morning, Hoop in the afternoon and ride bikes in the evenings before dark. This summer was shaping up to be one of the best ones ever. Every day was drenched in both sunshine and things to do. If I wasn't working, I was hanging out with my friends. Things were perfect. I truly felt like the best was yet to come. Seemed I could do no wrong. I only looked forward to things getting better and better as senior year approached.

1989: A Novella

July

July was hot as all get out. After the tropical storm passed through, each day was "Africa hot"! Instant sweat was to be expected each time you stepped outside, regardless of whether the sun was out or not. Bright sunny days with little cloud cover and clear moonlit nights that were humid and warm. These horrid conditions were a way of life and did not stop me and my friends from getting out and doing things.

As the Fourth of July approached, Macka and I would hang out when we could and we'd kick it with the neighbors up the street; some siblings from St. Croix in the Virgin Islands named Rawle and Shane,

Rawle and Shane came to the Lane a bit later as there was quite a bit of movement of West Indian families to the Houston area as they sought opportunities in the oil and gas industry.

I met Shane first when he was just a toddler. One day I was sitting under the carport at home when out of nowhere a baby, clad in only a diaper, came walking from the back of the house. He proceeded to walk through the breezeway to the step where I was sitting. I couldn't help but wonder where in the hell did this child come from? I figured that someone would come looking for him so I played with him until his mama, who was extremely panicked, came and got him. That incident lead me to meeting his family and his siblings, Rawle, in particular.

1989: A Novella

Rawle was stoic and took no shit from anyone. He didn't say a lot and when he did, it was direct and to the point most of the time. Once when we were a bit younger, we all decided to try some things to make some money together and form a club. We chose to sell wholesale greeting cards that we found in the back of a comic book.

We decided that the club needed officers, and I was nominated to be the president. As fate would have it, I received the most votes. I swelled with pride as I was younger. They really respected me and were willing to follow my lead.

Well, Rawle wasn't willing.

"No one younger than me gon' tell me wha' ta do"

"I got the most votes, so I'm the president."

Rawle stood to his feet and repeated his sentence
"No one younger than me gon' tell me wha' ta do"

I wasn't scared of Rawle, but he was definitely scary. He wanted to kick my ass; I wasn't about to back down without giving him a piece of my mind.

As I stood up and prepared to tell him that I was gonna tell him what to do as I was elected fair and square…

I couldn't even inhale and form my lips into the first word of the sentence because Rawle scooped me up and body slammed me to the hardwood floor.

1989: A Novella

BAM!!

Everyone jumped up in shock. Somehow, some way, I jumped up off the floor like a cat on a hot tin roof throwing punches and trying to punch Rawle in the face. No punches landed as Macka and Bam Bam restrained me.

I wanted to cuss him so bad, but my breath. There was none. I was inhaling but there was no exhale. My body was trying to recalibrate and remember how to function. That took a minute even though it seemed like time stood still.

I steeled myself.

Teary eyed, I stood up straight and stared at Rawle in his emotionless smirk.

I walked toward him, just one step, a very cautious step, and I took a measured swallow as I was breathing again.

"I'm still the president."

Shocked by my audacity, he just stared at me.

Oddly we all became super tight after that. Bonded by a body slam. Life has a funny way about it.

The 4th seemed like it was our last holiday as kids on Allen Lane. Macka, Bam Bam, Rawle, Mario, and I were out, preparing to light up the street.

My Pops hooked me up with a ton of fireworks and we started off the evening popping firecrackers.

1989: A Novella

We'd hold them in our hand and throw him at the last minute like little grenades. We'd put them in soda cans, wedging them in the opening that you'd normally use to drink from the can and we'd hold it high in the air to feel the slight kick from the pop. Jumping jacks were lit and thrown in the air where they were prone to whizzing in any random direction. Any old toys were used as props for the miniature explosions.

As darkness enveloped McNair we'd set off a barrage of bottle rockets and Roman candles.

Shane took some time to play with my little brother who was running around with sparklers.

As the night was coming to an end, we were preparing to light entire packs of firecrackers and revel in the barrage pops, bangs, and cracks that they would make.

Bam Bam decided that wasn't enough. He had been quiet for a bit but we didn't notice.

He was taking the gunpowder from a pack of firecrackers by slitting the side and scraping it into a pill bottle. The child proof cap had a little hole in the top and a stem was placed in the hole to ignite the pill bottle.

"Holy shit Bam! That's like a bomb!", I could barely contain my excitement.

Bam Bam nodded as he was finishing scraping gunpowder into the pill bottle.

1989: A Novella

After a cacophony of firecrackers and Roman candles, the bomb was finally finished.

The excitement was bubbling up like oatmeal when you don't monitor the heat and it starts to boil out of the pot.

We were all so happy to set the pill bottle off and there was one problem. Where? Where would we put it to detonate it?

Mario wanted to put it in the ditch inside of the concrete culvert.

Everyone else vetoed that immediately.

We needed a place where it could be lit while being able to get away from it.

Bam Bam took it upon himself to put it in Macka's mailbox. Before anyone could think of a different location, he made a beeline to the mailbox and opened it up. He sat the pill bottle on the hatch.

I yelled, "Light it nigga!"

We all laughed.

"I need a new stem!"

Bam Bam said this in the most dramatic way possible. You would have thought that this dude was about to perform surgery.

1989: A Novella

Rawle lit a stem and gave it to him. Bam Bam took it and blew the tip to stoke the heat. The tip glowed like a firefly in the humid July night.

Moving rapidly, you could tell how nervous Bam Bam was as the stems light shook in the darkness.

We all looked for places to take cover.

"Light it nigga!"

We all cackled.

Macka, Mario, and I were peeking over the side of my dad's pickup as we looked across the street at Rawle and Bam Bam by the mailbox.

Rawle assumed the "getting ready to get the hell on" position. He was ready to make the dash to safety as soon as the pill bottle was lit.

Bam Bam decided to move the pill bottle inside the mailbox.

Facing the opening he had one hand on the hatch and he held the lighting stem in the other. We could see it flickering back and forth nonstop; Bam was nervous. He was scared.

It was too late to turn back. Trembling, he moved the stem toward the powdered fuse…

1989: A Novella

I ducked down and about three seconds later I heard the mailbox hatch slam shut and the sounds of running on asphalt.

BOOOOM!!!!

The explosion was loud! I ducked and covered my head.

Silence.

I heard nothing in the aftermath. The dogs stopped barking and the crickets stopped cricketing. The bullfrogs went silent.

After what seemed like an eternity, it was probably closer to five seconds, I raised my head up to see Bam Bam and Rawle emerging from the ditch in front of the house that was owned by the Greens.

We all went back into the middle of the street.

Everyone was still stunned by what happened. Mario broke the silence.

"That shit was loud", Mario was looking to and fro as he spoke.

"Hell yeah!", was my co-sign as I approached Macka's house, specifically the mailbox.

"Dawg! The mailbox gone!"

1989: A Novella

The mailbox had disappeared. The only thing left was the pole that supported it.

It was literally blown up.

Everyone started laughing and cracking up. The mailbox was blown up!

We had to listen to Bam Bam talk about how fast he ran to dive in the ditch. We laughed.

Rawle didn't even know how he got over by my yard.

"I used all my speed and into the ditch I jumped!"

We laughed.

We continued to laugh until we realized that Macka was probably going to get in trouble for the missing mailbox.

Macka stared into space for a second.

He looked at Bam Bam.

The silence was so uncomfortable.

"Damn Macka he blew your shit to smithereens!"

My comedic relief had everyone, including Macka smiling and laughing in the middle of the street.

Soon reality set in and Macka was going to have to answer for that mailbox. Wherever it was.

1989: A Novella

I got up the next morning, ironically to put some bills in the mailbox for my parents, when I looked at the pole that once held up a mailbox.

Something said look up.

I looked up and turned a bit more toward Macka's house and on the roof, laying on the shingles, was the mailbox. It was laying there flat as if someone peeled it open.

It seemed like that was the last bit of summer excitement. Summer was getting boring as my older friends were embracing adulthood. They were working. A couple were also preparing for the military.

I began to think that these had to be the proverbial dog days of summer. The days and nights held the kind of heat that made the air feel thick and damp above the steaming hot blacktop, like the road was mad at the sky for trying to melt it back into tar and gravel. My days were split between working at the mall, hanging out with the fellas, and lying across my bed, letting the box fan do its best to keep me cool.

But those times with my boys? That's what I lived for. We'd post up for hours playing Nintendo. *Tecmo Bowl*, *Double Dribble*, and *Mike Tyson's Punch-Out!!* were the games of choice. Talking trash was required especially if you lost and had to pass the stick. When we weren't glued to the screen, we were outside hoopin'. Games of H-O-R-S-E or 21 in my driveway, or we'd hit the park for a full run if we decided to head that way. Some days we just rode our

1989: A Novella

bikes through the neighborhood, chasing nothing in particular but feeling like we had the world in our hands.

And when we weren't moving, we were roasting; playing the dozens, cracking jokes, daring somebody to laugh. That's where I thickened my skin, I became a straight up assassin with the punchlines and a master of the poker face. Somebody always ended up mad, but in the end, everybody knew it was love.

That was the rhythm back then—work, jokes, games, and that slow grind of surviving the summer one sweaty, hilarious day at a time.

When the day was done and it was time to come in, I'd collapse onto my bed, journal in hand. The pen moved almost on its own, spilling out poems and half-finished raps that felt deep in the moment—though I knew some of them would make me cringe later. I wrote about everything: the way sunlight kissed the rooftops at dusk, the hush that followed a thunderstorm, and always, the girls. I kept a top-ten list that shifted constantly—sometimes daily, always weekly. Some made the cut because of a smile, others because of how they wore their hair, or how they laughed like everything I said was funny. It wasn't about any one thing; it was the possibility they carried.

The nights in July stretched long and wide, almost daring me to sit with my thoughts. I'd lie there, staring at the ceiling, pen tapping against the page, playing out conversations that would probably never happen. I'd write those too—part poetry, part daydream—trying to capture something I couldn't quite name. Whatever it was, it felt just out of reach, hanging there in the thick summer air.

1989: A Novella

And yet, even with all that restless energy, there was a shift coming. I couldn't explain it, but I felt it in the stillness of the nights, in the way the days seemed to drag and speed up all at once. Something was waiting, and it wasn't going to be the easy kind of waiting. It was the kind that changed things, whether you were ready or not.

1989: A Novella

1989: A Novella

August

The days of August came heavy with heat and the kind of restless energy that hung in the air like a warning. Summer had been good so far—the Juneteenth festivities, Fourth of July fireworks, along with afternoons and evenings spent at the mall working part-time hours to stack a little cash. I wanted more. I needed more. LL and I had been talking all summer about how to come up, but we hadn't figured out how yet. The mall was only getting me so far and LL wasn't working. Despite our efforts to stay busy and to stay positive, the streets were calling us. There were kids in the 'hood who were making some serious money selling drugs.

I told LL about what happened the other day at my grandma's house. She lived right at the intersection of Harrison and Broad, and her house faced Broad and the aptly nicknamed "Burtwell's Corner", where a nightclub/upstairs apartment was owned by the corner's name sake. While the building was torn down, there was a strange rock that was on the corner that was McNair's unofficial landmark. That rock was McNair, and in a strange way it defined us; oddly beautiful, strong, and defiant; standing out in the middle of all things.

I was at my Grandma's, with my cousins Fred, Rod and Tye. We all grew up near each other; literally right around the corner and we were like brothers. On this particular day, an older dude named Gary came through and was hanging out with us in my Grandma's driveway. He was cool and always showed a young fella like me love. It was an ordinary day, and Gary came up the block from

1989: A Novella

Frenchtown and started talking to Fred. I wasn't paying attention to what Fred and Gary were talking about, I was just hanging out watching the people pass by.

Every now and then a car would pass by and Gary would say, "I'll be back" and then he would jump in the car and make the block. He did this a few times and after the second or third time, I saw him put a twenty-dollar bill in his sock.

I said nothing, but I was paying attention.

It happened again several times over the course of an hour. As Gary got out of the last vehicle and prepared to put a 20-dollar bill in his sock, the sock was bulging with money, at least 200 dollars in twenties was crammed in there and covered by his wind pants.

I said nothing.

Gary was laughing as we were trying to throw a rock up to hit the water tower and hear the ping that it would make. Fred and Gary continued to make some small talk. After a few minutes, Gary prepared to head back toward Frenchtown. That's when it happened; I saw the source of the twenty-dollar bills.

He reached into the pocket of his wind pants and pulled out a pill bottle. He twisted off the top of the pill bottle and poured some off-white-colored cubes in his hand and took a rough count of how many there were before cupping his hand to make sure they all got back in the bottle before resealing it.

1989: A Novella

As Gary walked away, he said, "I'm out, let me get to the house."

Fred said "Alright boy, let me know what you wanna do."

I said "Alright G"

Gary nodded at me as he disappeared up the street.

I couldn't shake the event from my brain and I would think of it from time to time. That was easy money. I also thought that there had to be a catch, because it all seemed so easy. The realities were in direct conflict with each other. On one hand, I wanted to have money and buy myself nice things. I wanted to be able to have the independence afforded to a person who has financial security. At the same time, I could never sell a drug to people and be responsible for destroying their lives. There were too many people around the way that I was connected to who became a shell of themselves due to their addiction to crack cocaine. Plus, I didn't want to go to prison. I would be a disappointment to my whole family, not to mention that the penitentiary doesn't seem very enjoyable. That would be a terrible place to spend any part of my life, even if it was for a day.

Yet, the streets and all of its allure was always lurking. Beckoning me to join and be a part of it.

LL and I would talk about these things and he would agree that it would not be in our best interests, so we tried our best to move on from the thought. We might not have been hustlers, but we found our way into the streets and hung

1989: A Novella

out on the cut from time to time. There wasn't much else to do.

I didn't see Macka much. He was working quite a bit as July ended and August began. He was a dishwasher at Ryan's Steakhouse and he had been working a lot of hours. One day before the upcoming weekend he was off. I was outside shooting some hoops and he came outside.

It was in the late evening as the sun was about to set, and I walked across the street to his house.

"What's up man?" was my greeting as we dapped each other up.

"Chillin'" was his reply. Something seemed a bit off, but I didn't pay it much attention.

"You been working a lot, homeboy!"

"Yeah man, they got me closing almost every night."

"Damn, I wish I was getting your kind of hours. I ain't trying to wash all them damn dishes though, I do that enough at home."

Macka told me I was stupid as he cracked a half smile.

We headed to the backyard to sit in the chinaberry tree. That was where we hung out and talked. When we were little kids, we'd grab the two branches while simultaneously walking up the trunk to do a backflip before going up and sitting on the branches. Today I felt like doing that flip and I don't know why. Perhaps it was because we weren't little kids anymore. The arc of our lives was

40

1989: A Novella

shifting, and change was afoot. Macka seemed to be feeling that way more than I did. I was genuinely excited that my friends had graduated and that my senior year was right around the corner.

"I don't want to move, man." Macka took a chinaberry off of a branch and threw it in the yard.

I had a leaf and I pulled off each side of it, leaving only a stem in between my fingers. I rubbed it between my fingers and then placed it in my mouth. It hung off the corner of my mouth like the milk straws at school.

"Dawg, why don't you just stay here with your brothers?" I just wanted him to see that this was an option. At least it seemed like it was.

Macka just stared into space, quiet. A pained look appeared on his face.

"Why you trippin? It's not like you'd be far away if you did move."

"I don't want to move."

"Shit man, I don't know what to tell ya."

We just sat there in silence.

LL Called me the next day and told me that we had some girls to meet up with at the mall.

"Who? When?"

I was about to pepper my boy up with all the questions.

1989: A Novella

LL said, "Chill out mayne! They some girls I know named Sheka and Meka. They're twins."

"Twins? How in the hell did you meet some twins?"

LL chuckled.

"Don't worry about all that nigga, we just need to get a ride to the mall."

I was excited, "When?"

"Tomorrow" was the reply.

"Thursday? Who in the hell goes on a date on a damn Thursday fool?"

LL let out a heavy sigh, he was getting irritated.

"Let's find a ride and chill with all the questions. Trust me, the shit gonna be all the way live."

"Word up mayne!" was my reply.

"Ask Macka."

"I'm gonna ask him and call you back."

I called his house and he wasn't inside. I decided to walk out and see what he was up to. I went to the front door and I saw him outside.

"Yeeeah Macka!"

"What up" was his reply.

1989: A Novella

"Man, I need a big favor. LL hooked us up with these twins and we need to get to the mall so we can take them out."

Macka, looking vexed, just stared.

I stared back and said, "Can you just drop us off?"

"I gotta work."

"Cool." was my reply as I tried to find something in the yard to look at.

Eventually, I asked him, "Do you have to work tonight?"

"Naw", was his reply.

I decided that there wasn't anything else to say, so I went home and called LL back.

As soon as LL picked up, I said, "He trippin' man. We need to find another way."

"What's wrong with Macka?"

"I don't know, he ain't talking to me."

"What you mean?"

"What you think I mean? He acting like he mad or something. I went over there and asked him if he could take us to the mall to meet the girls. told him we were going out with twins and he acted like they should have been triplets so he could go too!"

LL laughed and I did too.

1989: A Novella

I straightened up a bit. "Seriously though homeboy, Macka been trippin for real!"

It didn't help that the double date was a disaster.

We went to the mall with my Mama. She had to pick up something at Sears, so she dropped us off at The Market and then she pulled around to the store, where she always parked. I lied and told her we had a ride home. I couldn't have my mama picking me and LL up from our date.

"Kirven, LL…" My mama called us by name as we prepared to get out of the car. I knew what was coming.

"Yall be careful in that mall. Don't let nobody touch ya weenie or ya booty!"

Grinning from ear to ear, LL and I both said, "Yes Ma'am!" As we exited the car went inside the Market. Sitting at a table by the elevator and stairs were Sheka and Meka.

The Market was a surprisingly hyped place that night. There were quite a few people who were there to see the latest superhero movie. The spot was buzzing, a symphony of clashing conversations and the rhythmic beeping of arcade games in Yesterdays. It was supposed to be a double date where we would grab a little food and then check out the movie. For LL and me, it was rapidly turning into a disaster of unparalleled proportions. Sheka and Meka, identical twins down to the asymmetrical bobs – Meka's was short on the left, Sheka's on the right – sat across from each other, looking very beautiful. Two cocoa brown honeys that were radiating an air of… well, I wasn't sure what it was, but it definitely wasn't enthusiasm. They

44

were full of attitude for whatever reason. I couldn't understand that. LL and I had just cut our hair, the flat tops were freshly faded and our fits were definitely on point.

We stepped to the table and we all greeted each other. After that there was a period of silence. The uncomfortable kind. Never a stranger to socializing, this was a new moment for me.

"So," I forced some conversation, trying to break the ice. "You ladies excited for that new superhero movie?"

Meka, my date, shrugged, staring through me. She might have been people watching or figuring out how to ditch me, I wasn't sure.

She sucked her teeth. "I heard the reviews are bad."

Sheka, LL's date, didn't even look up. "I'm only here for the popcorn."

After a bit of awkward conversation, LL went to get us something to eat.

LL, upon his return, tried to lay on the charm as he came back with some pizza.

"You guys like pizza? I got a large pepperoni."

Both twins wrinkled their noses simultaneously. The twin synergy was in full play here.

"Ew, pepperoni?" Sheka said, finally making eye contact with LL, a look of mild disgust on her face. "I'm really not trying to eat no white people pizza."

1989: A Novella

Meka also decided to let him know he made a bad decision. "Damn, you got pepperoni nigga?"

This was not going well at all.

The pizza sat untouched, a greasy monument to our failing date. I tried to make small talk with Meka about school, but her responses were monosyllabic and punctuated by long, awkward silences. Meanwhile, LL was trying to engage Sheka in a conversation about music, but she seemed more interested in rolling her eyes and checking her reflection in her compact mirror.

Things escalated when LL, in an attempt to get his mack on, put his arm around Sheka. Meka's eyes narrowed.

"Um, LL?" she said, her voice dripping with ice. "You need to not be all up on my sister."

I quickly changed my mind about being a mack myself and I just chilled. I was ready to play defense just in case the twins tried to attack my boy.

LL blinked, staring with a shocked look on his face. "I was just... you know..."

"Yeah, I know," Meka interrupted. "You're all up on her. It's wack."

Sheka, who had been silent until then, chimed in, "Totally wack nigga."

LL's face went from shock to anger. "I was just trying to be nice!"

1989: A Novella

"Nice is buying her a slushie, not... that," Meka gestured vaguely with her hand, as if LL's arm was some kind of contagious disease.

A full-blown argument erupted, with LL defending his actions and Meka accusing him of being inappropriate. Sheka, seemingly bored with the whole thing, just stared at me ready for me to say something so she could snap on me. I sat there, mortified, thinking about running up the stairs to escape and disappear.

Suddenly, Meka stood up. "Come on, Sheka," she said, her voice sharp.

Sheka, without a word, stood straight up and followed her sister. They left the untouched pizza, sodas, and the two of us sitting in stunned silence. The twins marched out of the food court, their matching bobs swaying in perfect, synchronized indignation. LL and I exchanged a look that said it all: Worst. Double. Date. Ever.

I don't even want to know how in the hell we ended up in the situation, but there we were in the middle of the market looking crazy. On the bright side, we were still going to see the movie. We bought our tickets and we waited for the movie to start by going back to The Market and looking for some different girls to talk to.

Things couldn't get any worse I thought. I wanted to go and get a drink from Orange Julius and chill until we could go into the movies and find a good seat. I didn't notice the guy walking in the opposite direction.

1989: A Novella

The air in the mall was thick with the scent of corn dog batter and cheap perfume. I was heading towards the theater, minding my own business, when *bam* – a shoulder slammed into mine. I stumbled, nearly dropping my Orange Julius. I turned to see a guy built like a brick outhouse, wearing a hat and cowboy boots.

"Hey, watch where you're going boy," he drawled, his voice thick with southeast Texas twang.

"What?" I retorted, not appreciating the attitude. "You watch! You bumped into *me*, I ain't your boy."

He ripped off his shirt and squared up. He was cut up with a big snake tattoo that covered one of his pecs.

Being skinny and bird chested, I kept my shirt on. There was no way I was going to run. That giant son of a bitch only gave me one option.

I put my Orange Julius on a nearby table, squaring up and staring as intensely as I could. I was scared to death but my furled brow and face said otherwise.

He stepped closer, his eyes narrowing. "Whatcha gonna do…boy?"

"Say, I ain't gonna be naan 'nother boy!" I replied, fear turning into anger.

He cracked a slight smile, and in a low, menacing tone he said. "Let's go nigger."

OH HELL NAW! I was pissed. I clenched my fists tighter and I was ready to fight this dude that I had no chance of defeating should he grab me or try to grapple with me. I only boxed, threw hands…

And with that, he stepped to me and threw a punch. He was aiming to knock me out and he telegraphed his punch. I ducked, his huge fist whistling past my ear, and countered with a quick jab to his ribs. He grunted and doubled over, surprised by my quickness. I squared up, bouncing on my toes, ready to box. This dude was bigger than me, but I wasn't about to back down.

He rushed me, like Reggie White rushing a quarterback. I lost my footing and stumbled back, landing hard in the corner by Chick Fil A. This was the moment I feared. I'm small and trapped in a corner by a big ass cowboy. I tried to regain my footing but I found myself doing an impromptu wall squat, keeping my guard up and avoiding the haymakers he was throwing my way. Suddenly, that kicker reared back his booted foot, clearly wanting to cram it in my face. I tucked my chin into my chest, raising my arms and fists to guard myself like a boxer in a more traditional stance.

His boot connected, not with my face, but the crown of my head. Stars exploded in my vision. I felt like a cartoon character who had an anvil dropped on them! I staggered out of the corner, dazed and disoriented, but still ready to scrap. I squared up once more, ready for whatever. What I needed was help, I needed relief and as I emerged from that corner, I saw a couple of friends from the hood, Malik and Carlos and they merely stared. I was a bit too dazed to get mad. I had to just get myself together.

1989: A Novella

Suddenly, somebody came in with a quickness. It was LL! He came out of nowhere and *crack*! A right hook connected with the side of the cowboy's head; the punch snapped his head back. The cowboy crumpled to the ground like a sack of potatoes, a thin line of blood appearing above his eye.

At that moment, LL and I didn't hesitate. We pounced on him, a flurry of kicks and punches raining down. Adrenaline surged through me; it energized me and gave me strength - a mix of fear and fury. The two-man rat pack was in full effect.

"Who's the boy now?"

"Who's the nigger now?"

LL and I were just kicking and stomping him wherever we could at this point.

Just as I was about to deliver a particularly satisfying kick to the cowboy's ribs, a whistle blew. Mall security came running up, looking less than thrilled. Swarming us, they grabbed me and LL, ready to escort us out of the mall.

"Hold up!" a voice yelled. It was one of the kids who worked at Foot Locker, near where the fight started. "That cowboy attacked him! He started it!"

Other voices chimed in, backing up the story. Because I worked at the mall, and because of the corroborating witnesses, the security guards let us go. They gave us a stern warning and told us to go to the movies.

1989: A Novella

We never saw the cowboy again. The last we saw of him, he was curled up in a fetal position in front of Yesterday's, moaning softly. LL and I, victorious, triumphant, buzzing with adrenaline, went to see the latest superhero flick. There was a strange mix of guilt and triumph swirling in my stomach as LL and I sat on the very front row of a full theater watching the movie. My head hurt and I never had such a bad time watching a great movie.

I would be forever grateful to LL for having my back. He could have just tried to break it up and not have that dude hit me anymore, but he came with the intent of whooping that dude's ass. I would never be able to repay him for that. As long as we lived, I'd have his back and he would have mine.

It sucked that he wouldn't be at school with us in a few weeks. He was banished to the Special Assignment Clinic for that last day of school egg-throwing incident, which was later deemed starting a riot. He would be there our entire senior year.

After the movie we hitched a ride home with Jerome. He was at the movie and lived a street over from me on Wheat Lane. Jerome was a year younger than us, but he carried himself like he was older than his years. He was cool and laid back, the kind of dude that was always solid and never got caught up in any nonsense. He didn't ask questions when LL and I hopped into the ride, he just took us back to the hood. On the way to McNair, we talked about the movie and when we got to the intersection of Harrison and Broad, Jerome dropped us off before making a left and heading toward Wheat Lane.

1989: A Novella

As I got out of the car, I told Jerome that, "I think Prince should have been in the movie, he did all the songs".

He laughed and gave me some dap.

LL excited and said, "Thanks for bringing us home, Jerome"

"Yeah, thanks", I co-signed.

As we prepared to walk across the street to Allen Lane, it felt like the night could have gone on forever. The streetlights buzzed; moths were circling their glow. The night air was still except for the hum of Jerome's engine as he drove away.

The evening was nuts! A bad date, and a fight all in the same night. Never mind that we almost got kicked out of the mall and could have missed out on the greatest superhero movie ever.

We didn't even make it to the other side of the intersection as seemingly out of nowhere a car emerged from the north end of Harrison and slowed down.

"Yo! Y'all got anything?" a voice called out from the passenger side.

LL shook his head. "Nah, man, we ain't got nothing."

The car rolled off, but before we could take another step, another one pulled up. And then another. Three cars in total, each one asking the same question in different ways. The words hit the air heavy, rang in our ears at a different frequency; like they were testing us. It was like someone was waiting to see if we'd fold. My hands balled into fists at my sides, not out of anger but out of something deeper, something like fear, I'd even say a sense of dread. It wasn't the first time, and I knew it wouldn't be the last. I tried to ignore that and just chalk it up to this hood life we were living.

When the last car disappeared down the street, LL and I laughed it off, but I looked at him as I knew he was thinking what I was thinking.

"Mayne we could have had sixty dollars", I said while stepping across Harrison and hitting The Lane.

He replied, "That's crazy KOT."

I could see something shift in his eyes. We walked down the street in silence. the weight of the moment settling between us.

When we got to the front of my house, I prepared to go inside and LL prepared to go through Macka's yard and go home. On this night it felt bigger than just splitting up to go inside. LL slapped me on the back, gave me a quick nod, and cut through Macka's yard, hopping the fence like he'd done a thousand times before. I watched him go, his silhouette disappearing into the darkness, and turned left toward my yard so that I could enter the carport and go inside.

Two roads, one choice. I wasn't naive enough to think that one night changed everything, but it felt like it. LL's path wasn't mine, and deep down, I knew it never would be. Still, as I stood there, the weight of that intersection

1989: A Novella

pressed down on me. It was the last time the summer felt simple. From here on, nothing would be the same.

That night stuck with me, more than I wanted it to. I couldn't shake the weight of it. There was something about the way LL's silhouette disappeared into the dark like a choice I wasn't ready to make. I told myself I'd forget about it. I'd wake up, play some video games, maybe shoot some hoops, try to call a girl who wouldn't call me back. But the weekend had other plans.

By Saturday, the whole neighborhood felt empty. LL wasn't around. Nobody was. The phone barely rang. The usual spots—Speedy's, The Front, the park, and even The Market—felt hollow, like everyone else had somewhere to be except me. I flipped through my top ten list of girls, crossed off two for not answering my calls, and added a new one just to keep the list moving. I turned on the TV, watched the same reruns, let the ceiling fan hypnotize me, and wondered why the weekend felt so damn long.

Sunday came slow and heavy. Mama didn't even have to tell me; I knew we were going to church.

It was the kind of morning where the clouds hovered low, quiet and thick in the sky, like they had seen something that couldn't be unseen. The sky's clouds looked heavy with tears they refused to shed, holding back rain like a secret too painful to release. I felt tension in the air, as if the sky was trying to warn me, but didn't know how.

We rolled up to McGowen Temple like always, the parking lot full of cars, with some parked across the street at the fire station. The day was going to be long. I settled into my

1989: A Novella

usual spot for Sunday school. We took turns reading the scriptures and talking about their meaning. We reviewed the question in our book and prepared to say the things we learned in class to the congregation. First the elementary group, then the secondary group, which I was a part of and then the pastor reviewed the adult lesson.

In between Sunday school and 11:00 service we got a break where we would go to the church cafeteria and eat cookies and punch. It was a time for us to basically have a recess. Normally I'd be talking and joking a bit, but I wasn't quite in the mood. I just wanted to go home and chill. I couldn't tell you what it was, but I wasn't feeling what was going on at church.

During testimony service, where we would praise the lord by singing old hymns, members of the congregation would stand up and give thanks to the Lord for all of the blessings that he had bestowed upon them. The same few ladies gave their testimonies and began to do their holy dances. I had them memorized and I was reciting in my head which part of the testimony was coming up next for each lady that danced. This was usually high entertainment during family gatherings as I memorized almost every "Old Saint's" testimony and holy dance. Today I was kind of bored. I literally wasn't feeling it. I went to the restroom, came back out and went back to I took my seat, half-listening to the choir, waiting for the service to end as it seemed to droll on and on...

Then Pastor Jenkins got up to preach the sermon, and something in his voice made me sit up.

1989: A Novella

"You better come on in the Lord's house!" he extolled, his voice filling every corner of that sanctuary and the end of his phrases and sentences were punctuated by a little double hop. "'Cause one day *hop hop*, you're gonna find yourself standing at a door that won't open *hop hop*. One day *hop hop*, you're gonna wish *hop hop* you had stepped inside before it was too late! *hop hop*"

The way he said it sent a chill down my spine. It wasn't just the words. It was the way his son, the organist, played low behind him, crescendos hitting at just the right moments, and his grandson doing the same with the drum set. It was the way the old folks nodded, the way the saints hummed and said "Amen". I don't know why, but for the first time that morning, I was really listening.

When Pastor Jenkins concluded and finished in a frenzy that got the saints up on their feet showing that they were sanctified and filled with the Holy Ghost, I felt something. I felt goosebumps on my skin. At the same time, Missionary Blake stood up with her tambourine and started playing and singing:

"You better come on in the Lord's house, It's gonna rain;

"You better come on in the Lord's House, It's gonna rain!"

Tears streamed down my face. I felt the spirit. I felt like I needed to just lay on my face and cry out to the Lord. I wanted to come into His house. I wanted to feel that "hedge of protection" that I always heard about. The Holy Ghost was in that church and I felt it.

1989: A Novella

That feeling didn't shake even after we left, even after I changed out of my church clothes and went back to staring at the ceiling. I thought about Reverend Jenkins' sermon. Something about the way he said it stuck with me. It felt like a warning, like somebody somewhere was about to be too late for something. Like it was about to rain.

It was a confirmation of my Mama getting on me about doing the things that I was supposed to be doing and not out doing things that would put me in harm's way.

The Pastor said that we needed to come on in the Lord's house before it was too late. I didn't know it then, but the next ten days were going to make him seem downright prophetic.

After a Monday of game shows, soap operas, and talk shows, I woke up the next day needing a ride to work. My first instinct was to call Macka, but he was a notoriously late sleeper. I also hadn't seen or heard from him since before LL and I had that horrible double date experience and fight at the Mall, so I needed another option. I called My cousin Walter, whose car put the hoop in Hooptie. He said he would give me a ride but it meant that I'd have to leave almost an hour earlier than I needed to be at work because he drove so slowly. I know that the car was in such bad shape that it couldn't go fast if it wanted to. At the appointed time, I got in the car with Cousin Walter and he took me to work.

Work was awesome. It was just a great day. I had fun with my co-workers and we were working the floor so I didn't have to unload merchandise off the truck. All I had to do was help customers, keep the jeans wall looking good and

1989: A Novella

keep the clothes on the rounder in my area finger spaced. When I took my breaks, it seemed like all my people were at work. I got to go down and talk to them a little bit. Walking up and down that mall some days I felt like I owned it. I felt blessed to work there and know people. I knew that I'd be able to work there until track season started and then I could come back and work in the summer. I also found out that I'd be able to work more hours in the fall, as I didn't have to stay after for track practice until the spring semester. It wasn't drug money, but I'd have a little more cash in my pocket.

My mom came and picked me up from work and I told her how good my day was. We continued to make small talk about my day, about hers, about her soap opera where rich people fought over a cosmetics empire like it was life or death. I nodded along, letting her words fill the space. It was just another ride home. Riding up the feeder, because Mama never drove on the freeway, passing King's Colony and eventually coming over the tracks into the hood. Everything was normal and good.

Until it wasn't.

When we turned onto Allen Lane, something felt off. The street, usually so familiar, stretched unnaturally long, like I was seeing it through a warped lens. The crowd on the right side of the street caught my eye first—people standing in tight clusters, their voices hushed but urgent. Then I saw the ambulance, parked a little further up, lights flashing against the darkening sky.

Mama pulled into the driveway and killed the engine. She didn't say anything, but I could feel her watching me.

58

1989: A Novella

I went inside, put my things down, and was about to step back out when a heavy knock at the door stopped me.

A Harris County Sheriff's Deputy stood there, his face unreadable, the kind of expression cops wear when they have to tell you something you can't unhear.

"You know Macka?" he asked.

I swallowed. "Yeah… why?"

He studied me, like he was measuring whether to tell me the truth or not. "Had he seemed different lately? Sad?"

The question sat in my chest like a weight. I thought back—Macka had been pissed about moving. He didn't want to leave, didn't want to start over somewhere else. He acted like he was pissed when I told him about the double date that me and LL had. I hadn't spoken to him since then. It had been a few days.

"He was sad about moving," I said finally. "He didn't wanna go."

The deputy gave a small nod, then left me standing there with my stomach twisting into knots.

I stepped outside, crossed the street, drawn toward the crowd like a current pulling me under. The murmurs turned into words, words into facts, facts into something too heavy to carry.

Macka was gone.

He shot himself.

1989: A Novella

A rifle. To the chest.

I don't even remember how or when I sat down, but suddenly I was sitting in the grass, knees up, arms draped over them, head hanging. My mind was scrambling, searching for loopholes, ways this could be wrong. But there weren't any. How could I make this unfortunate reality unreal?

A weight settled over me, thick and suffocating.

My cousin Tomur came and sat beside me. He didn't say a word, just draped an arm over my shoulder, grounding me when I felt like I was floating somewhere between disbelief and grief.

The street still looked too long, like I'd stepped into some alternate version of my life where things like this happened. But I knew it wasn't some dream I could wake up from.

It was real.

And nothing about this street, this summer, this life—was ever going back to the way it was before.

The immediate aftermath is a blur. Somehow I ended up at the park with my friends. When we arrived, we just kind of stood in front of the cars and were just in our feelings. We cried. We exchanged daps and hugs. There was such a heavy air of sadness. Macka was gone. He was dead. It seemed that for the longest time there was silence.

It seemed as though the universe aligned with our grief as Phil Collins' *In the Air Tonight* came blasting from Rod's

1989: A Novella

Mustang. That song—one of Macka's favorite songs—felt like the hymn we needed, a calling, a final embrace from something bigger than us. We stood together, the FTP, bound in silence, our hearts heavy with loss. Tears slipped down my face, warmed by the humid and hot night air, each drop carrying a memory, a piece of the past that could never be reclaimed.

As the song swelled toward its drum-laden climax, I tilted my head back, staring up at the vast sky, where the constellations we used to identify, blinked like a thousand quiet witnesses to our pain. I could almost see him up there, laughing, arms crossed, that half-smirk of his expecting me to say or do something to make him break first like I always did during our seemingly never-ending childhood activities and adventures.

I thought about us at six and seven, racing die-cast cars on the tracks that we made in the brick flower bed on the west side of my house, our voices ringing with excitement. The afternoons that were spent lost in battle with action figures, dreaming up alternate storylines as only we could. The scraped knees from makeshift bike ramps, the spectacular plays from playing football in the backyard, the reckless joy of being young and invincible—before we knew that time would become a thief that could betray us at any given moment.

But time *had* betrayed us. And now, at seventeen, I stood there mourning a friend who should have been standing beside me, arms crossed, smirking like always. Instead, he was gone.

1989: A Novella

I just wanted to remember the good times. Because remembering was all I had left.

I went home and once I took a bath; I went to my room and grabbed my journal. My 6-year-old brother, Rhari, sensing that something was wrong, came and hugged me.

"I love you Kirv."

"I love you too."

"Macka died?"

"Yeah, he died today."

He then disappeared from the room without a care in the world. I don't even know why he was up and about because it was kind of late. For a little troublemaker, he was very protective of me. Oh, how I wished I was 6. I wasn't and the one care that I had was crushing me under its weight. As I prepared to write, the words came free and easily as I succinctly summed up what happened.

I wrote, "I never thought that I would have to write anything like this, but my best friend Macka killed himself today."

I stared at the pages, tracing the words that led up to the post. My Top 10 list. The bad date. Fight night. And then, the mention—so small, so easy to overlook—that Macka and I hadn't talked.

I thought back to this morning. The morning before everything changed. I needed a ride to work. I could have asked him. *I should have asked him.* But I didn't. I assumed he was sleeping, and I let it go. A simple choice,

1989: A Novella

a passing moment that meant nothing at the time—until now, when it meant everything.

If I had knocked on his door, if I had made that call, if I had just *checked in*... he would probably still be alive. That thought burrowed into me, deep and relentless. I could have saved him. I could have stopped this from happening.

But I didn't.

And now, I would have to carry that weight forever.

I was a pallbearer at the funeral.

That morning when we gathered at the church. Someone made us some black elastic arm bands that had the white letters, "FTP", ironed on them. I slipped it on my right arm and lined up with my guys to enter the church behind the casket. We walked down the main aisle and sat in the front row. AJ, Mario, Bam Bam, James, Todd, and myself solemnly listened to all of the songs and the announcements. Everything became a blur. I couldn't tell you what I said during the allotted time for remembrance. I couldn't tell you anything about the service or the eulogy; It's just a giant mish-mash of sadness. I can remember being at the cemetery; after the prayer and the "ashes to ashes, dust to dust", each member of the FTP took off their armbands and placed them on the casket to be buried forever. While the FTP was not done, it would never be the same. The placement of those armbands on the casket was symbolic of a time that was not only special, but of a time that had run its course. The Flat Top Posse wasn't disbanding as much as reorganizing.

1989: A Novella

Everyone got together after the funeral and we started to talk about things that we could do as a crew for the rest of the summer. It was just about time for AJ and Todd to leave for basic training. Rod, James, Patrick, and some of the others were working and LL, Wade and I were going back to school for our Senior Year. LoLo was bringing up the rear as a Junior. This would be our swan song for the summer. Ultimately, we decided to go to the beach on Saturday.

I have to admit this stirred up some excitement in me as this would be some welcome activity where we could go to Galveston and just hang out. We'd enjoy the beach and start to adjust to life without our anchor, the guy who held us all together. Most of us hung out because of Macka. With the exception of LL, AJ, and LoLo, none of the crew lived in the hood, they mostly lived in Baytown. Rod and James lived in Highlands. Mario lived in La Marque and was in McNair for every break and holiday. As we were planning out our Galveston trip, I was reminded of the times that we would sneak away to Houston and go to a club called The Rhinestone.

I didn't realize it at the time, but The Rhinestone was not in the best part of the city of Houston. Tidwell and Parker, or at least the area surrounding it had a bit of a reputation for crime and nefarious activity, so one of the first times we went, gunfire broke out while we were waiting in line. We were all ushered in and asked if we were drinking tonight as it was safer to herd everyone inside instead of getting shot.

I didn't drink or smoke because I didn't like either, but I took that band because it made me look older if I had the

1989: A Novella

21 and up band on my arm. Not sure if I could have ever looked as old as I wanted to anyway with my baby face and peach fuzz on my top lip. I was 17 and didn't have to shave; the exception being when my Dad thought he saw a bit of darkness on my lip and then I'd be ordered to "shave that shit off my lip".

But on this night, me and the fellas had on our 21 y/o arm bands except for LoLo who just looked too young. He was barely 16 and they wouldn't let him in. He had to wait in the car. In that parking lot. The one where they were shooting.

It was exciting going in there. After you paid, you had to get searched and go through a pat down to make sure that you didn't have any weapons or illegal items. After that you went through a blacked-out entry way into the club and all of the fun that you could handle. We'd spend a lot of time circling the club like vultures as we looked for dance partners. Trying to find someone to dance with was tough sledding. Maybe I didn't look old enough, or maybe they thought I couldn't dance. Either way, I heard "no" enough times to build some character, some resilience. That would always change once the DJ got on the mic and prepped the crowd for the Harlem Shuffle. His name was Captain Jack and would always get things started by saying his catchphrase "Don't Do It Like that Baby!" and playing the song "Clear" by Cybotron. He would then chant "I wanna lay some pipe, pipe tonight, pipe tonight' and everyone would be singing along. Then he would segway into the "Harlem Shuffle" and we would do the accompanying dance for about an hour as he changed up the groove with songs from popular artists like Michael Jackson and Maze.

1989: A Novella

The final hour would begin with a couple of slow jams and then more dancing until the lights came on at 2am. My curfew was usually about 12:30 and I stayed in trouble as I would break that any and every time we went out there. I learned that if I just asked to spend the night at Macka's house, there wasn't going to be an issue!

I smiled as I reminisced and headed home. This beach trip was going to be the perfect way to end what was once a promising summer. It was now turned on its proverbial head and there was nothing I could do about it, but enjoy the rest of it.

Friday came and I was looking forward to the weekend beginning. I worked Friday morning and was very excited about the trip to the beach. I was sitting at home watching "Woody Woodpecker" when the phone rang. I walked over to the bar and grabbed the receiver off the hook.

"Hello?"

"KO!"

"What's up?" It was AJ and he was excited.

"I'm Chillin, watching cartoons.", I replied.

AJ wanted me to go kick it with them. CeCe from Oak Addition, Kim from Old Baytown, and some other girls were gonna be hanging out with James, Pat, Todd, and some others.

"Naw, man. If I go with y'all tonight, I won't be able to go to the beach tomorrow."

1989: A Novella

We chit-chatted some more and he agreed that the beach would be the best choice since we would be there all day and plus it was the beach.

"That's cool KO, because you know i'm gonna wash the 'Stang in the morning and we gonna have all the car freaks jockin'"

"Word up! You already know! I got us a tape made and everythang!"

"Word."

We said our goodbyes and I hung up the phone to finish watching some cartoons. The one where the Droopy is the sheep herder and the wolf is the cow herder is on. I sat on the couch laughing at all the antics until the final show went off. Soon after my Mama came home. She was going to make burgers and fries for us, as she always made some sort of fun food on Friday. The only thing I hated was the aftermath because I was going to have to wash the dishes. It was going to be totally worth it this time because I would have chores done and I would be able to go to the beach. The only thing I'd have to do was cut the grass Saturday morning and I would be free to roll out with AJ and the homies to Galveston.

Mama was still cooking and I watched the news until I saw Marvin Zindler tell me who in Houston had slime in the ice machine. I went outside for a bit. It was hard going outside and knowing that Macka wasn't there. It was hard going outside and seeing the flattened mailbox on the roof of his house. It had been up there for over a month now. I just went out and sat in the bed of my dad's old pickup. Soon,

1989: A Novella

LL and LoLo saw me and they came across the fence and through Macka's yard to join me. We sat and talked amongst ourselves for a bit. I asked them what they were doing tonight and LoLo said he was going inside to watch "That's Incredible" along with the other Friday night TV shows. He was gonna go to his Daddy's house in Louisiana in the morning and come back on Sunday. LL said he was gonna hang out on Godfrey and he couldn't roll tomorrow because he had some things to do. We hung outside a lil longer and then I was summoned by my mama and that meant that the food was ready. I went inside and ate my cheeseburger and crinkle fries. I washed it down with some homemade punch so sweet, red residue remained inside the cup.

After a bath, I settled down on the couch to watch some Friday night television. I watched the two brothers in the orange car with the rebel flag on top outwit the crooked mayor and his minions, the goofy sheriff and deputy, while racing down dirt roads and jumping bridges that were out. Never has there been a county before or since that had so many obstacles such as broken bridges and roads under construction. After that I watched the shady Texas oil tycoon wheel and deal his way into all types of drama and chaos. The last show before the news was one where a couple moved to an idyllic subdivision in California and in the midst of all the well-manicured lawns and seemingly happy people, adultery and deception lurked. These TV shows gave a person all the drama and excitement they could handle on a Friday night!

One thing about this August Friday night - It was HOT. I was on the couch in the living room trying to get cool. The

1989: A Novella

air conditioner and box fan were struggling to keep the place cool. Things were even worse in my room. So I decided to sleep on the couch, occasionally trying to put my legs up on the wood paneling to cool off. That idea sounded great in theory, but it wasn't working.

As I lay on the couch that night, my mind was on the beach—on what fun it would be to hang out with the crew one last time before life pulled us all in different directions. I was desperate for sleep, but the heat was relentless, the a/c and box fan barely stirring the suffocating air. I lay there tossing and turning, feeling a strange unease settling in my chest. It gnawed at me—a bad feeling I couldn't shake, though I didn't know why.

Then, at some god-awful hour, the phone rang.

It was mounted on the wall, just a few feet from where I was lying, its deliberate, sharp ring cutting through the silence like an omen. I refused to answer it. Something in me already knew I didn't want to hear whatever was on the other end.

It kept ringing. Once. Twice. Ten times. Maybe a hundred.

I just laid there. Tossing. Turning.

Finally, my Mama came from her bedroom, her footsteps heavy in the stillness, and answered it herself.

I held my breath, listening. I knew—*I knew*—nothing good ever came from a phone call at that hour.

And I was right.

1989: A Novella

She said, "I think you better tell him." Her voice was steady but heavy, like she was holding back something too big to say all at once. Then AJ's voice came through the line.

"KO… James, Todd, CeCe, and Pat had a wreck. Todd didn't make it."

I stood there, gripping the phone, my body frozen in stunned disbelief. My mind struggled to catch up with the words. Todd. *Gone.* Just ten days after losing Macka, I had lost another friend. Another piece of my world shattered in an instant.

AJ kept talking, filling in the details, but it was like I was hearing it from underwater—his words muffled and distant. James had been driving his car down East James, taking the back road behind the apartments where the street turned into Kilgore Road. He was going too fast, and when the road dog-legged to the left, the car hit loose gravel and skidded off the pavement. They flew through a ditch and slammed into a tree. The impact crushed the passenger side, hitting hardest in the backseat—right where Todd was sitting.

He didn't stand a chance. He was gone before the EMTs could even arrive.

Everyone else survived, bruised, battered, and scarred, but still breathing. CeCe walked away without a scratch— the only one wearing a seatbelt. I should've been relieved for her, grateful that she was spared. But all I could focus on was Todd. Todd, who had just graduated high school. Todd, who was counting down the days until he left for basic training. He was so proud to be joining the Marines,

1989: A Novella

ready to take on the world. He had a whole future stretched out in front of him—adventure, purpose, something bigger than this small town.

Just like that, the future was gone.

I don't even remember getting off the phone with AJ. One moment, I was standing there holding it, and the next, I was sinking into the weight of it all. Dread. Grief. Rage at how unfair life could be.

I felt like I was drowning in it. Ten days. Just ten days since Macka, and now Todd is gone, too. Another friend I couldn't save. Another goodbye I never got to say.

The memories came rushing in too fast—Todd's bright and toothy smile, the quarter miler who had a way of making sure we'd make the medal stand, his great sense of humor and endless confidence that things were always going to work out. I thought about how we used to sit around talking about the future, making plans that felt so solid, so *real*.

Now, those plans were just ghosts.

I couldn't help but think that it could have been me. I could have been with them.

The thought hit me like a punch to the gut.

They had invited me to go with them. If I had said yes, I would've been in that car. I would've been sitting right there with them, laughing, cracking jokes, never imagining that a tree waited at the end of that curve.

1989: A Novella

But I didn't go. I didn't go because I had made plans to go to the beach with everyone, and my Mama wasn't about me running the roads all weekend. The beach was supposed to be a celebration—one last hurrah before everyone started going their separate ways. So I made the choice to stay home. The choice to ride to the beach on Saturday…that ride, that beach trip, would never happen.

Instead, I stood there holding the phone, thinking about how easily it could've been my name AJ said. My body crushed. My Mama would have answered a different call in the middle of the night, and she would have been devastated by the news that came from the receiver's speaker. Seems I made the right choice in staying home.

Now I had to attend another funeral.

I had lost two best friends in the span of ten days. Two funerals. Two caskets carried by kids barely old enough to vote; hell, I still couldn't vote. Both times, I stood there as a pallbearer, my hands gripping the cold metal of the handles, helping to carry friends to a hole in the ground when they had been full of life just days before. Fresh out of high school, they should have been planning their futures—college, the military, road trips, anything *but this*.

It was August 1989. School would start right after Labor Day, but it felt like the world had already moved on and left me behind. Time blurred. Days stretched into each other, difficult and heavy. I was just going through the motions, showing up but never fully present. Every moment felt like it was happening in slow motion and it seemed like I was looking through cheap plastic wrap, making everything hazy with grief.

1989: A Novella

My friends and cousins tried to help, but what could they say? Most of them hadn't lost anyone, let alone two best friends in ten days. My mama and my aunties looked at me with that mix of pity and uncertainty, like they weren't sure if they should say something or just leave me alone. I didn't want to talk about it. I didn't want to *feel* anything. My uncles continued to talk trash and that normally entertaining conversation between them may as well have been silence. My dad, in between shifts, would make sure that I was busy. I'd help him bleed the brakes on the car or make some other repair. That would usually go left because he lacked patience when he would call on me to get some tool that I never heard of.

"Kirven go in that lil house and get me them channel locks."

I didn't know the wrench that you could adjust with a roll of the thumb was called "channel locks". If they would have just been called an adjustable wrench or something, I would have probably become a mechanic. Instead, I got in trouble and there was frustration all around.

I kept moving, though. One foot in front of the other. I showed up where I was supposed to be; work, school, the usual hangouts. Everything felt muted, like the world was a song playing through broken headphones, where I recognized the songs but melodies were muted.

But then, there was Angela.

She came out of nowhere, like a sliver of light breaking through a dark room. We met during those long, empty weeks, and from that moment we started talking, we became friends and something shifted. She had this way of making things feel lighter, like the weight on my shoulders wasn't quite as crushing when I was around her and her friends.

It wasn't anything dramatic or over-the-top. Just little moments that reminded me life hadn't completely stopped. The way she smiled, the sound of her laugh, she was just a cool person to kick it with. LL and I would end up over at her apartment. She lived with her mother, father, and little sister at the apartments at the end of East James; ironically about a mile or so from where Todd died in the car wreck. We'd be over there hanging out, laughing and talking. It felt good to be around a group of people where LL and I didn't share our grief, we only shared fun times. There were times when we would go over there and the apartment would be full of kids - It was just a good environment for LL and I to be in. I thought it was weird that no parents were around much, but hey, I wasn't complaining.

I didn't expect to feel anything *good* after what had happened. I didn't expect to be clowning like I used to but as the days passed, I started to feel better about life and the possibility of having a future. I found myself looking forward to seeing her, to hearing her voice. For the first time in weeks, something felt alive again. After a few conversations on the phone, I kind of started falling for Angela.

I was smitten, and it caught me off guard. I didn't know if it was because I needed something…*someone* to pull me out of the fog, or if it was just Angela herself. But I didn't care. In the middle of all that darkness, she became the bright spot I hadn't realized I was desperate for.

74

1989: A Novella

She didn't erase the grief. Nothing could. But she made it bearable. She reminded me there was still something worth holding on to.

And for that, I was grateful.

One afternoon I went over there and she was home with her sister, Tedrah. We were talking and hanging out as usual and we ended up in her room. New Edition's "NE Heartbreak" was in the tape deck. I flipped it over to side two while we were talking. After a little mundane conversation, things got quiet as "Superlady" played in the background.

Angela smiled at me.

I stared back.

I broke the silence. "You know it's been cool kickin' it with you."

She smiled and said, "I like hanging out with you."

I thought about all the times Mario and I talked about aspectness and this was the first time that I could truly put it to the test.

As I reached toward her, I grabbed her hand and stared a bit more intently.

"I hope we can continue. I have plans."

Demurely, she smiled.

"What kind of plans?"

1989: A Novella

I moved in a bit closer and steadied myself for a kiss. I thought my heart was going to pop out of my chest as the sax from "Competition" filled the silence in the room.

"These plans..." I leaned in and kissed her on the lips.

There was no resistance as our lips touched. It was a kiss that bordered between a peck and a French kiss. She backed away just a bit to look at me. She smiled and put her arms around my neck. I took my arms and pulled her in closer, our foreheads touching. I kissed her again.

New Edition serenaded us with "Coming Home".

This time we were in full make out mode. Our lips began a dance of passionate exploration as we got to know each other intimately. Her lips felt as if they were tailor made to be kissed by me. The press and pause of our kisses became rhythmic as if we were choreographing them to Ralph and Johnny's crooning. Eventually, I moved my tongue to a position where hers would meet mine in slow and methodical, yet tantalizing and passionate exploration.

I pushed her back so that I could position myself on top of her and when I did, we looked into each other's eyes in a moment of pure connection. We continued to lay on the bed and make out.

Things were getting pretty intense when we metaphorically came up for air.

"I think we'd better stop." Angela looked at me, her eyes soft from the light of the sunset coming in through the window and its blinds.

1989: A Novella

She was right. Even though we were laying on her bed, fully clothed, the passion and sensuality made me feel like I'd made love to her, or at least what I thought making love would be like.

I gave her a kiss and said, "OK."

I sat up on the edge of the bed. Angela laid there looking at me.

"Are you mad at me?"

I tried not to look incredulous, I just had one of the best experiences of my life and this girl wanted to know if I was mad at her. I immediately went into my aspectness bag.

"I can't be mad at you when we just shared something special."

She smiled. I smiled back.

I think this was one of those things that signified some maturity or whatever Johnny said.

My journal entry that night was one that said that I had "made love" and Angela shot up to the top of the top 10 list. It wasn't going to last.

It was a great moment, but Angela and I didn't last. I didn't have a car and I think that she would have grown tired of the inconsistency of my presence. By the time school had started, we were still cool and everything, but I didn't go over there as much and eventually I wouldn't see her at all. I just started to believe that I was bad luck with the ladies when it came to trying to settle down and be in a relationship.

School was starting soon and all I could think about to distract myself was girls. I had plenty of girl friends but I wanted a *girlfriend*. Macka's brother had a girlfriend and I talked to her little sister for a short time but right before school started, we were done. Mainly due to immaturity and stupidity; my immaturity and stupidity. We remained friends and kind of talked off and on through the school year.

LL had been MIA. I hadn't seen too much of him and he had been hanging a bit more with some of the homies who hustled. He was trying to prepare himself to spend his senior year in SAC. Of all the things that could put a damper on a senior year, spending the whole year off campus in a silent room while in a 3 walled study carrel, definitely does the trick. I was listless.

The best thing that could happen to me after the summer was returning to Sterling High for my senior year. Wade and I talked about what we were going to do for the start of school. I gave him a call.

"What up Dubb?"

"What up Kirv?"

We exchanged pleasantries and talked about the coming school year.

"Say mayne, I ain't never been this ready for school to start", came from my whole chest as we started chatting about all things senior year.

1989: A Novella

I could feel Wade nodding through the phone.

"I can't wait Kirv, the FTP will be in full effect!"

"Oh we gonna be back fa sho".

We continued back and forth for a while discussing all things senior year. We talked about the females, we talked about track season. Talked about having the best senior year we could have and we wanted to start the year off right. We were trying to figure out the one thing that would start the school year off on a good note.

I thought for a minute as Wade told me about a couple of the girls he wanted to holler at when school started.

Suddenly, I interrupted him.

"Yo, let's dress up for the first week!"

"We can wear some old clothes from the 70s!", he replied.

"Hell yeah! We can say we're freshmen!"

I told him, "My Daddy got some old school butterfly collar shit in the closet!"

"OOOOH OOOO!" came through the phone.

"I can get some of my Daddy's clothes too!"

It was settled, we were going to dress up like "freshmen". This made the anticipation of starting school almost unbearable. It was going to be the funnest day of school ever. It would be just the thing to help with taking my mind off the tumultuous summer and beginning the look forward

1989: A Novella

as graduation would only be 8 months away. June 1, 1990 was going to be a day of epic proportions.

September

Labor Day came and went. My Mama and Daddy prepared BBQ with all the fixin's: Chicken, Ribs, Sausage, Hot Dogs, and Meat Patties. Potato Salad and Pork N' Beans as the sides. All the white bread I could handle. We feasted like royalty, sitting around the table with plates stacked high, wiping our fingers on napkins that didn't stand a chance against the sauce.

"Mmm! Daddy, I swear you put something extra in this sauce this time," I said, licking my fingers.

"You know I did," he said with a knowing grin. "Gotta keep y'all on your toes. Secret ingredient."

Mama scoffed. "Ain't no secret. He can't tell you the ingredients, but I bet I know who can."

I blurted out, "Jesus?"

My Mama tried not to laugh as we were all cracking up.

"Boy hush! Go on and let him think he a magician, ask him who makes the mop sauce!"

We looked at Daddy and he said nothing, but his face said the answer that Mama wanted everyone to know.

We all laughed as Daddy nodded sagely. "That's right. A magician never reveals his tricks." The man acted like he didn't just confirm that the secret sauce was Mama's mop.

The conversation drifted as we passed plates, sopped up sauce with slices of white bread, and declared—more than

1989: A Novella

once—that we couldn't eat another bite, only to somehow make room for more.

After we were sufficiently fat full, I found my second wind. I never could sit still when family was over. Before it got too late in the evening, I ended up doing what I did best— entertaining the house with my antics and shenanigans. It usually involved dancing and being silly, but my real talent was imitating people.

That night, as the grown folks leaned back, satisfied from all of that good eating, I launched into one of my greatest hits—Prince. Despite my absolute lack of singing ability, I had mastered the art of sounding like him. I'd tilt my head back, squint my eyes like I was feeling every note deep in my soul, and let out a perfect Prince falsetto:

"Until the end of time, I'll be there for you; you are my heart and mind, I truly adore you…"

My voice wavered dramatically, exaggerated just enough to have everyone hollering. My aunts clapped, my cousins fell out laughing, and Daddy shook his head, trying to hold back a grin.

"You ain't got no business soundin' like that," he said, as he shook his head and feigned stabbing me with a rib bone.

But I wasn't done. I'd throw my hands in the air like I was summoning spirits, drop to the ground and do a sexy push up and crawl, and belt out *Scandalous*, complete with the dramatic wails and all.

1989: A Novella

Mama wiped tears from her eyes from laughing so hard. "Boy, you crazy."

Crazy or not, I had my audience. That's all I needed. It felt good to get that energy out and set the mood for school the next day.

Once we finished up, packed plates, and cleaned up the kitchen, they headed home. Everyone had work and school the next day. I went to the bathroom, shaped up the high top fade, and prepared for bed. Wade and I had spread the news about dressing up in 70s clothes and wearing it to school. I laid out my first day of school outfit and admired it for its brilliance.

Red polyester bell bottoms, a purple shirt with a butterfly collar featuring a wide assortment of multi-colored dots, and a brown suit jacket with cream lapels. It was epically hideous and an awful combination for an outfit. I knew it was going to be a hit.

As I got ready for bed, my thoughts drifted to Macka and Todd. It was still hard to wrap my head around the fact that I had friends—barely 18—who were already gone. I didn't know if I'd ever understand why God allowed it. A wave of sadness hit me, and then I thought about LL. He wouldn't be starting senior year with me tomorrow. Instead, he'd be reporting for his SAC assignment—ironically, at the Green Center, right across from RSS. Even more ironic, it used to be "The Skate Machine," a place once filled with laughter and music, now repurposed into a holding spot for students in serious trouble. It stung knowing LL wouldn't be walking the halls with us, cracking jokes and flirting with the girls. I missed my dude already. As I lay in bed, those thoughts circled in my mind—but so did the possibilities. Something about senior year felt like it could be the best chapter yet.

After the events of the summer. That was what I needed. Something that I *had* to have.

I left my house and instinctively looked toward Macka's house. His car sat in the driveway. I took a second glance and walked up the lane to Harrison. I walked across the street toward broad and took my seat on the rock which was located on Burtwell's Corner. I was a senior without a car. I had tried my hardest to get my Mama to get me one, but it didn't happen. I continued to hope that it would happen when I turned 18. So for the time being I rode the yellow dog. While it certainly wasn't cool to be a senior riding the bus, there was enough of us who did, so it didn't matter. Being a "yella dog" riding senior had its perks. I usually hitched rides with friends when I could, but when I took the bus, I had my pick of seats—all the way in the back on regular days, warm and up front when the cold hit. I still had fun riding too. Sometimes, the simple things are the best things.

Everyone who came to the bus stop was overwhelmed by my outfit. Reva, Shellie, and Tashia looked stunned. They didn't know what to think as I was dressed in my 70s attire, with my high-top fade immaculately cut. Everyone at the bus stop and the two that followed were tripping out on my outfit. I got on the bus and Miss Yolanda looked at me and actually cracked a smile. I knew I was official then.

The drive to RSS felt quick as we took Harrison, then consecutive left turns onto Jones and Thompson Roads.

1989: A Novella

After picking up Gertie on the I-10 feeder and crossing Wade Road, we exited to get my cousin Wendy before heading up John Martin Road. Leaving McNair always felt like entering a different world, a stark contrast to places like Baytown. The drive from John Martin to Cedar Bayou Lynchburg and then Bush offered a rapid transition from rural to small-city life. Passing Cedar Ridge Apartments on Bush, where Todd had lived, brought a pang of sadness at his absence.

As Bus19 approached the high school, excitement started to build. We passed the church and the old skating rink that was now SAC and made the left into the school's driveway. I got off the bus and proceeded to walk past the art rooms and down the main corridor into The Commons.

The Commons was the morning neighborhood of the school, a social map etched in routine. On the right, in front of the trophy case, stood the McNair wall—home base for my people. The jocks claimed their turf in front of the mirror, checking their reflections like gladiators before battle. To their right, the Linus kids held court. A crew of girls from different neighborhoods posted up next to them, followed by the preppy boys and girls, always polished and put-together. The OBT kids staked their claim beyond them. The FTP had our own spot—our column—wedged between the jocks and the girls' crew. Scattered throughout were other kids, floating between groups, but the main players were clear. The RSS ecosystem was on full display. The Stars and the Ag kids had their own territories elsewhere on campus, their presence felt even if they weren't in the Commons.

1989: A Novella

Every morning followed the same pattern. I'd hit the McNair wall first, chilling with my people, before making my rounds—acknowledging the jocks, then sliding over to my spot with the FTP. But today was different. Today, I had *the outfit on*. And the moment I stepped into the Commons, I felt it—the shift. Stares lingered a little too long. Conversations dipped into hushed murmurs. A ripple of curiosity moved through the crowd as I passed.

By the time I reached my spot, it had turned into a full-blown sideshow. My boys were already locked in, waiting to dissect the moment. Then Wade rolled up, grinning, ready to add fuel to the fire.

Kids didn't know what to think as everyone was gathering around laughing and talking to Wade and I about our outfits.

Marcus was one of the first to see us. "Say mayne, what the hell y'all got on?!" he said, half-laughing, half in shock.

I grinned, spreading my arms wide like I was on a runway. "70s fashion, my brother. We freshmen today. Y'all just ain't ready."

The jocks by the mirror started cracking up, nudging each other.

"Oh nah, Kirv and Wade came through with the *full* outfits on today!" One of them, Plick, pointed at my shoes. "Look at this dude! He got the old school working!"

"Tell me you didn't iron them pants *just* for this moment," said Eric, one of the Linus kids, shaking his head.

1989: A Novella

I kept it cool, brushing invisible lint off my sleeve. "This polyester, ain't no need for ironing!"

By the time I reached the FTP column, the crowd was already hyped. Wade strolled up, took one look at me, and just lost it.

"My man, you ain't just step out—you *arrived!* You look like a damn album cover!"

"Legendary," someone muttered behind me.

"Man, you know I had to hit 'em with something special today," I said, adjusting my butterfly collar, playing it up.

Wade circled me like a coach assessing his star player. "OOO OOOOOH! Bro, this ain't just a fit. This is a *moment.* We witnessing history."

"You stylin' too dawg!" Wade had on some polyester bell bottoms and a butterfly collared shirt of his own.

A couple of the girls from the neighborhood crew walked over, grinning.

"We need to know," Nisha said, hand on her hip. "Did y'all plan these days in advance, or did y'all just wake up and *decide* to bless us?"

"The people needed something to talk about," I said, flashing a confident smirk. "Consider it a public service."

The crowd erupted.

"Boy, y'all *love* attention," one of the preppy kids called out.

1989: A Novella

"Nah," I shot back, and simultaneously Wade and I said, "Attention loves *us*!"

Laughter, dap, jokes flying from all corners. Wade threw his arm around my shoulders, still shaking his head.

"I swear, bruh. They ain't ready! We're the only ones who could pull this off."

And just like that, the Commons belonged to us and the FTP on the first day of school.

After the morning spectacle in the Commons, the bell rang, sending everybody off in different directions. Wade and I took our time, moving through the halls like we owned them.

"So I heard that Brittany is in our first period class…is that true?" Wade asked as we strolled toward first period.

I thought about the possibilities for a second, then shrugged. "I hope so, she fine as hell!" I went on to ask him, "Since it's the first day of school, am I actually late or just *technically* late?"

"Technically," he smirked.

"Then I'm good. They better not try to give me a tardy!"

We both knew that wasn't going to happen. We never got in that type of trouble. Some teachers found me entertaining, but others? Not so much. There was no in between. As I headed to English, I prepared myself for Mr. Gordon to be one who would be firmly in the ranks of the

1989: A Novella

"Not so much crowd. He was older and had a reputation for being a bit crotchety.

I slid into class just as Mr. Gordon, standing at the podium and taking himself way too seriously, was clearing his throat. He gave me *the look* over his glasses.

"Ah, you must be Kirven. How nice of you to join us."

"Thank you, sir, it's great to be here in your esteemed class" I said, giving him my best *model student* smile as I slid into my seat.

Most of the class started giggling and stifling laughs as I sat and tried to get my materials together. Wade, already seated, muttered sarcastically, "There you go," under his breath as he gave me some dap.

Mr. Gordon sighed and pointed to the board. "We're discussing symbolism in *The Great Gatsby*. Care to enlighten us on the green light?"

I leaned back, then I sat up straight and sighed like he did, feigning the same irritation. "The green light is the dream, right? Gatsby keeps reaching for it, but he never quite gets there."

Mr. Gordon raised an eyebrow. "And what does that tell us about the American Dream?"

I gave a half-smile. "That it's more like a crack pipe, er… pipe dream."

The room *erupted.* Even Mr. Gordon had to chuckle, though he quickly covered it with a cough.

1989: A Novella

"While I appreciate your… succinctness, perhaps a more nuanced answer next time?"

"I'll work on it," I said, opening my notebook like I was about to take *very serious* notes.

Wade nudged me and whispered, "Yeeeah Kirv O'Nealuh!"

"Yeeeeah Jeffrey Wadeuh!," I whispered back.

Such was the way of our world. It was truly a stage and we wanted to entertain. I wasn't sure if Gordon was going to allow it or not. But he seemed genuinely amused when we tried speaking in iambic pentameter and using the vernacular of the Middle Ages in regular conversation. It was also cathartic to be back in school, going to class, talking to friends and having a sense of normalcy. I truly believed as the day went on, that the school year was going to be one of the best ever.

As the first week of school progressed and we started wearing normal clothes, I began to set my sights on the important things at school, like the girls.

I had met a girl in the first days of school and her name was Jaye. She was a cutie with smooth brown skin and beautiful light brown eyes, a shade in the middle of brown and Hazel. She was kind and sweet, the type of girl I always want to meet! So I set my sights on her and tried to figure out how to approach her.

I figured I should just write her a note:

Dear Jaye,

1989: A Novella

What's up?

I was just sitting in class and decided to write you a note. I don't want to go to track practice today. Off season sucks and coach be having us running long distance! Do you like Coach Seale? Dunlap is cool. What events are you running?

W/B/S

Kirven

I took my note and folded one corner over like I was getting ready to make a glider. Instead of folding the other side over, I folded the paper in half vertically and flipped it over. Then from the bottom I folded the note in thirds and tucked the pointy end into the note where only the point stuck out. I wrote "To Jaye" on the note and then wrote "Pull" on the point. My note was ready to be delivered.

The bell rang and Wade and I quickly went out to meet up with Adrian in the hall.

Adrian walks up and he is smiling so big that we know he has been up to something. We all greet each other with some daps and fake punches. Wade and I are like puppies as we can't wait to hear what's happened with our boy.

As we walk toward the commons, Adrian laughs heartily. "Ya boy done came up! I got Rochelle's number!

"Mack Daddy!" was my reply. We laughed.

Wade pushed Adrian playfully and said, "I see you Mayne!"

1989: A Novella

By this time the three of us were grinning from ear to ear and I had to regain my focus.

"Let me show y'all how a real mack do it!"

I flashed the note I had without revealing the name on it.

"Yo! Who you giving that to?"

Adrian tried to grab it from my hand so he could see who the note was for. I was quick enough to prevent him from grabbing it and then I pretended that I was Magic Johnson backing him down in the post so I could shoot the baby hook.

I shot the fake baby hook and told the fellas, "Watch ya boy work."

Jaye was in the commons talking to some of her friends when I made the bee line over to her. I busted up in between a couple of the girls and said, "What's up?"

Jaye smiled and her friends who were both amused and irritated by my arrival, returned my greeting.

A smattering of "hello" and "hi" came from the girls.

"I meant to interrupt because I have some business with Jaye...Don't worry, I won't be long."

Jaye smiled and was shocked. The girls looked at me like I forgot to put on deodorant. I gave Jaye the note and walked away. After about 3 steps I turned back and faced them all.

"Told y'all i wouldn't be long."

1989: A Novella

My heart was about to bust out of my chest as my nerves were trying to adjust to this random fit of boldness that I tended to have. I went over to the spot where Adrian and Wade were watching.

"Man you crazy!" Wade was looking at me, bemused.

Adrian laughed.

It was time for us to go to Algebra II..

Math was all about two things: staying under the radar and making sure I copied enough notes to fake my way through the homework. Mr. Francis didn't play. It was bad enough when you were keeping up, but If he caught you slacking, you were getting called on.

Halfway through class, I got caught slipping. Mr. Francis looked up from the board and locked onto me as I was getting ready to ask Twiila a question. I had no chance of playing it off.

"Kirven, what's the next step?"

I stared at the equation. It might as well have been hieroglyphics.

"Uh… distribute?"

He nodded. "Then?"

I hesitated. "Then we… collect like terms?"

Mr. Francis actually smiled. "So you *do* pay attention."

1989: A Novella

I winked and nodded enthusiastically. "Yes sir, as much as my classmates allow!"

Laugher erupted from the class. Mr. Francis shot us all a look and it got quiet as hell. The lesson resumed.

Wade, sitting behind me, whispered, "You lucky as hell."

"Like a mug." I whispered back.

Adrian leaned forward to whisper something to Marika.

Never slipping, Mr. Francis called Adrian to the board.

Lunch and the rest of the day flew by. Soon it was time for track class.

It felt so good to suit up and go out to the track. The team and I left out of the athletics area at the back of the school and went down the path toward the track to get the beginning of the year spill from Coach Dunlap.

Coach Dunlap was a legend. A southwest conference champion, he was an institution at RSS as his track program was one of the most successful in the state. He'd won many district championships and had sent many tracksters on to regional and state track meets. His 1st day of track practice speeches were legendary in my mind. He had a way of making us all feel important. He had a way of making us all feel that we had value. He made us believe that we would always be able to improve every meet.

"Alright men, listen up! Today is Day One. The start of something bigger than each of us. Some of you have been here before. You know what this is about. You know the work it takes. Some of you are new. Well, let me tell you—this ain't just about speed. This ain't just about running, It's about showing up and about pushing yourself further than you thought you could go. I don't care if you're the fastest guy out here or if you're still figuring out how to come out of the blocks—I care that you give me everything you've got. Every day. Every practice. Every meet.

You're going to have tough days. You're going to have days where you feel like you can't take another step. But that's when you dig deep. That's when you remember why you're here. You remember the team. You remember the pride."

Coach Dunlap paces a bit and looks at Wade and I. He follows that up with glances at the other upperclassmen.

"We're going to build something special here. We're going to build a team that supports each other, pushes each other, and celebrates each other's successes. We're going to build a legacy."

As he continues to pace and talk, he comes to a stop and smiles at us.

"One more thing men! Let's make this season one for the history books. Let's show them what RSS Track is all about. Because you will get better—every practice, every race. You will improve. And I promise you, by the end of this season, you won't recognize the runner you are today. Now, take a look around. These are your brothers. Your training partners. Your competition. The ones who are gonna push you when you think you've got nothing left. And it starts today. Right now!"

The excitement is palpable and this is just the beginning of the off season.

"Seniors Stretch 'em out!"

After track class we headed to the buses. On the way out to my bus, I saw Jaye. I smiled at her and before I could ask her when she was going to write me back, she smiled back at me and gave me a note folded into the same type of envelope like I gave her.

I said, "I'm gonna be able to call you later, right?"

She smiled coyly.

I took that as a yes as I hurried out to the bus.

When she was out of sight, I opened the note and it read:

Dear Kirven,

I'm glad that you wrote me. I don't like off season either. Coach Seale is cool, we don't practice as long as yall do. I think I'm gonna run the 100, 200, and maybe the relays. I don't know yet. W/B/S

Jaye

PS call me tonight

I almost blacked out from excitement! Jaye gave me her number and I definitely was going to call her after school. I kept thinking about how good we'd look together. She was so pretty and that smile of hers…something about a girl with braces. I was smitten. I might have skipped a little bit as I headed to the bus loading area.

The bus ride home after the first day was surprisingly normal for bus 19. We made our way home without incident. As the bus rolled up to the corner of Harrison and Broad. I jumped off with everyone and made a beeline to the house. As I entered the house, I put my things down and watched some cartoons for a minute. After about 30 minutes, the phone rang.

"What's up KOT?"

"LL! You home?"

"Yeah man."

"I'll be over there in a minute."

As soon as Woody Woodpecker pecked his last peck and laughed his signature laugh, I left the house and cut through Macka's yard while skillfully jumping the fence to go to LL's.

He's waiting for me at the back door.

"What up dawg?" I extend my hand to give him some dap.

"Shit, nothing man! How was the first day?" he replied as we completed the hand shake.

I replied "You first." as I tried my damnedest not to bust out laughing.

1989: A Novella

"You ain't right KOT! I was bored out of my mind. I can't lie though, the burritos be hittin'!"

We laughed.

I said, "Those are the same ones we have at school, right?"

He tried to convince me that the SAC burritos were better than the ones at school.

"Nigga, I'm trying to tell you that there is something about them that's different."

I smirked.

"One thing that I do know is that I ain't planning to find out if yo' ass telling the truth or not!"

We laughed and started being silly, when suddenly the front door popped open. LL's mama was home from work.

She was no joke. All laughter ceased as she crossed the threshold, stopping in the middle of the living room. I was sitting very relaxed on her couch.

LL exchanged the first greeting.

"Hey Mama."

She just glared at him.

"Hey Ms. Linda."

She glared at me too.

1989: A Novella

It may have been fifteen seconds in total but the silence seemed so long and it was so uncomfortable. I sat up. Slowly. Respectfully, or at least what I imagined what respectful sitting up would look like.

"Why is this house not clean, LL?"

He stood up but seemed to be frozen in fear.

"Why are you sitting on my couch, Kirven?"

I stood up. The frozen fear bug caught me too.

Get to cleaning my house LL!

He went to grab the broom to start sweeping the kitchen floor. Never mind the fact that it appeared to be spotless. He was sweeping.

"Don't just stand there Kirven! Get this mess cleaned up!"

I snapped out of my fear induced coma. Quickly, I went into the kitchen to run some dish water to wash the three or four dishes that were in the sink. I squirted in some detergent and agitated the water with my hand so that the bubbles would form faster.

Miss Linda went into her room emerging with a belt.

She glared at us. LL swept faster, I washed the dishes faster and thoroughly.

There was another sudden sound at the door and LL's older sister, Richie came in. She took one look at what was going on and was about to laugh. I think Miss Linda glared at her too because she didn't give us the business, she just hugged her mama and went into her room.

Meanwhile, Miss Linda took a seat on the couch as I finished the last dish and began wiping the counter top. LL got the dust pan and carefully dumped the little bit of dust in the trash can. We had finished the work in record time.

Miss Linda takes one last menacing glare in my direction.

"How's Betty doing, Kirven?"

"She's fine."

Miss Linda smiles broadly. We always participated in this "game" where Miss Linda - don't get me wrong; she was indeed tough and stern, would be on our asses like a crazy woman and then she'd become "normal" doting on us until she deemed something important enough that she needed to make a point and then...crazy woman.

She asked how was school and then gave LL all the daggers her eyes could muster. Deep heavy squints that would have killed the average kid, but LL just sighed.

"It was okay Miss Linda"

I didn't want to say anything else because I knew LL was going to have to live with being kicked out of school and his mama's wrath for a long time.

"Let's go to the back porch, Kirv. I need a fade."

"Word up."

Miss Linda sat up. Glared at us.

1989: A Novella

"Let me find some hair on that porch when you're done, hear?"

LL said, "ok".

She got louder.

"Did y'all hear me?"

As we went to the porch, I said "Word up!"

As I was about to cross the threshold to go from the house to the porch, I felt something whiz by my head and hit the door jamb. I hurriedly closed the door to scared to look back and see what was hurled in my direction.

Through a hearty laugh, I asked LL why his mama always doing us like that.

He just laughed and shook his head.

I got the clippers and oiled them up. Ever since I started growing the high-top fade, I learned how to cut my hair during my sophomore year. Macka's dad, Mr. C was the last person to cut my hair. I became something of an amateur barber and I would hook my friends up from time to time.

As I cut LL's hair, I told him all about school and all the happenings. He was genuinely curious about everything that went on, but I know it pained him to hear about school and he wasn't there. I sensed that and cut the stories short.

"Say man, I'm finna head to the house. Need to get on this homework."

1989: A Novella

LL smiled as he told me, "At least I don't have homework as I get all my shit done during the day...."

I smiled and told him that was a good thing.

"KOT, I need a favor."

"What's up?"

LL went in the house and came back out with a note.

"Give this to Risha for me."

I took the note. Risha was a girl at school that LL liked. He hadn't been able to see her since he was in SAC. I guess I was going to be LL's personal mailman.

"Word. Holla at ya boy!"

I stepped off the porch and prepared to hop the fence. As I prepared to grab the top bar of the cyclone fence I yelled, "Sweep that hair up, boy!"

LL laughed and gave me the finger.

I hopped the fence and stopped for a split second. So many conversations happened in the chinaberry tree in Macka's yard. I paused briefly to touch the trunk before walking through the yard and across the street to my house.

Everything I did reminded me of my friends, especially Macka. Seeing his car made it seem like he wasn't dead. It seemed like he was out of town. The reality was harsh and I tried to shake it off as I went inside and prepared for dinner and homework.

1989: A Novella

I gave my little brother Rhari a scuff and hugged Mama.

"What's for dinner Mama?"

"Wind Puddin'"

That was her standard answer when she wasn't cooking.

"You can make you a sandwich, there's some chips in there too."

I made an executive decision to eat after I did my homework and called Jaye.

Once my homework was done, I went and called Jaye. I don't know what it is about calling a girl this first time, but it can be nerve wracking. My palms were a bit sweaty, but I was able to utilize the phone's rotary dial with maximum accuracy and efficiency.

After what seemed like a very long time, the phone started ringing. I tried to take measured breaths to calm myself and not sound like a pervert on the phone. It stopped ringing and someone picked up.

It was a male voice. He had a West Indian accent.

It must have been her father I thought. That was never a big deal to me because I was taught to be a gentleman. My Mama and Daddy would kill me if I wasn't.

"Hello…"

I tried to gulp quietly before speaking.

"Hello, may I speak to Jaye please?"

1989: A Novella

Surely my McNair Eddie Haskell voice would do the trick...surely.

The voice, suddenly a bit deeper and much sterner, said something different. The West Indian accent grew significantly stronger and more pronounced.

"Who is this"

I replied, "Kirven"

Jaye's dad was not happy. His response was swift.

"Listen 'ere Kevin, Kelvin, or whatever your name is, Don' call muh house no more!"

He hung up in my face. I heard the receiver hit the handset holder with such force, the combined hit and subsequent click sounded like a boulder cracking.

I held my hand set away from my face and looked at it. "Damn", I thought, "He didn't have to do me like that".

I went and made a weenie sandwich with mustard and potato chips on the side and watched the show where the former pro baseball player becomes a housekeeper for the ad executive in Connecticut.

Evidently, Jaye got an earful herself. She was so embarrassed that we didn't speak for a while. When we did, it was just to speak or as a part of a group conversation. Damn the luck.

After this turn of events, it seemed that I was destined to go to my final homecoming alone. It wasn't that big of a deal because I always went to the dance without a date, but I just knew that I'd have a date as a senior.

1989: A Novella

1989: A Novella

Homecoming

Every day in English I had to hear Brittany talk about her boyfriend and how they were coming to homecoming together. It got on my nerves and for some reason, she always wanted to tell me about it.

Brittany, our beautiful head cheerleader, our class president, was dating Edward, One of the star players from our crosstown rival. I actually went to junior high with him and he was a cool dude, but I would take his place on homecoming night if I could.

It seemed like every other day, Brittany would say something about her and Edward for all to hear.

"Edward and I are going to look at dresses for homecoming."

I just looked. My buddy Gerard would be irritated and try his best to ignore her, but then all the girls would start talking about going to get their dresses and other accessories.

Feigning seriousness I said, "Can we please stick to English?"

Everyone stared at me. I looked incredulously at their non-verbal insinuations.

Wade, imitating the rapper who always wears the clock around his neck, said "Yo, yo! Later for him!"

1989: A Novella

We all laughed and Brittney shot Wade a look before laughing herself. We were all friends and she knew we meant no harm.

In the midst of all the fun, I had an idea...

As soon as I got home from school, I went to LLs house.

"Say L, I have an idea."

"What's up?"

"Come with me to the homecoming dance! Maybe we can get you in on the sneak tip!"

LL's interest was piqued.

"Do you think they will let me in?"

"Only one way to find out, homeboy!"

We dapped each other up and I headed home.

The days and weeks leading up to homecoming were a slog. The homecoming week seemed like it would never arrive and when it did everyone was very excited and looking forward to going. I had received some unexpected good news.

My Aunt Beverly said I could drive her car to the dance. I don't know how or why my Mama agreed but she did. I had no doubt at this point that homecoming was going to be the best day ever. LL and I were going to pull up in Auntie's 300 Z and we would have a great time dancing and hanging with our classmates.

1989: A Novella

The day before the dance, I came home from school and put my things up. I grabbed my bike and rode off the Lane and went up Broad Street. I passed the crack house and the water tower. Rode by Melvin Jr.'s house and past Verdinell. I went through the four way stop and passed the old Harlem Elementary. I turned left on Washington Street. Tiny and Kasandra were sitting out front with their mama. I waved at them and rode down to the dead end where Jake, Jessica, and Jason lived. At the end of the street was a small trail that snaked down and then up to the railroad tracks. The smell of the weeds and the foliage filled my nose as I passed through the trail. I walked my bike across the tracks and jumped back on when I left the embankment.

I rode across the grass to the area where a playground was. It was defined by a two-tiered rocket that you could climb in. I laid my bike down and climbed up to the second level. This was one of the places that Macka and I would come to and chill when we wanted to get away because kids weren't coming to the park to play like they used to.

I sat on the second level and looked toward McNair. The water tower that said "Welcome to McNair" seemed like it was being cradled by a cloud-filled fall sky. I could hear the traffic from the nearby interstate. I just sat. I was feeling overwhelmed. I needed my friend. I needed my wingman to talk to me but I could hear nothing.

I needed to know why he did what he did. I needed to know. I needed a sign. I got nothing. A tear ran down my cheek and the light fall breeze dried it up.

1989: A Novella

I thought life shouldn't be this crazy. Yet, it seemed like it was that crazy. I had to figure out how to survive. I had to figure out how to live. Live without fear. I'd be graduating soon and the more I thought about what I wanted to do and what I wanted to be, there was doubt that I would do anything but die and the only thing I could be was dead.

Nothing seems worth trying if I was doomed to die.

I sat and thought a bit more about it as the sun prepared to set on the western horizon. That was my cue to head home. I took my bike and went home the same way I came. When I got to the corner of Harrison and Broad. There was a lot of strange traffic. People driving around looking for drugs. It pissed me off.

By the time I ate, took a bath, and finished my homework, I was starting to feel better. I went to my room so I could listen to some music and I opened my journal.

The words wouldn't come. I couldn't compose a sentence. I couldn't even put a top 10 list together. No thoughts were worth writing down. I just listened to The Quiet Storm until I fell asleep.

It was Friday. The homecoming game was that night and the dance was tomorrow. There was excitement in the air and as I walked into the commons that morning there was a pep rally going on and the band had us all hyped up. The football players were working themselves into a frenzy and enjoyed watching Adrian and the rest of the team get hyped! All the activity made it easy for me to be low key and get my bearings. My morning classes took forever but when lunch came, I was myself again.

1989: A Novella

I slid into my usual spot with Wade and the FTP. The jocks had their table, the preppy kids had theirs, and the Stars—the drill team girls—held down the middle like royalty.

"Who you think gonna start something today?" Wade asked, biting into his burger.

"Probably Kyle," I said, pointing across the room at a dude sitting at the table with the jocks. Kyle was a football player. He played on the offensive line and the word was that he was going to do something crazy for game day.

Sure enough—

There was some commotion.

The jock table *exploded* with cheering and noise.

Kyle ripped off his shirt and stood up on a chair and started yelling.

"ROSS IS BOSS!!" He screamed while beating on his big belly like a bass drum.

Everyone started laughing and cheering. The "Ross is Boss" chant lasted for a good two minutes as Ms. Christian started getting irritated.

Lunch was always a show. Sometimes I got in on it. Other times I just enjoyed the fun and laughs. Today, though? I had a plan.

I stood up, cleared my throat, and slipped into *full performance mode.*

1989: A Novella

"Dearly beloved," I started, mimicking Prince's signature voice. "We are gathered here today... to witness the triumph of the Sterling Rangers over the Rayburn Texans! We will win! We will defeat them! I mimicked some of my pastor's signature moves

The cafeteria *lost it.* Claps, stomps, people banging on tables.

"Kirven, that's enough!" Ms. Christian, while laughing, insisted that I stop!

"Don't shut down the word, Ms. Christian!" I said, while pretending to have the Holy Ghost as I went back toward my seat.

On cue Wade came and draped my letterman over my shoulders and as I got ready to sit down, I threw the jacket off and got the Holy Ghost again.

By the time the bell rang, It felt like we had a whole church service. The only thing missing was us taking up an offering!

Needless to say nothing productive happened after lunch. Going to class was simply a formality. We spent the entirety of sixth and seventh periods recapping and watching reenactments of the lunch time activities. By the end of seventh period my stomach muscles ached and my cheeks hurt from laughing so much.

The last bell was like the national anthem of liberation. Everybody flooded the halls, dapping each other up, making plans, and still talking about the crazy lunch.

1989: A Novella

Wade and I headed toward the parking lot, as he got to drive his mama's car to school sometimes. We stood by the car, stretching like we had just completed some hard labor.

"Another day, another hustle," I said.

"And we survived," Wade added.

"Barely. Today was wild!"

We stood there for a second, watching the chaos of people heading home.

"What's the move?" Wade asked.

I smirked. "Same as always, whatever comes up."

He grinned. "It should be live after the game!"

I said, "Word.", as we fist bumped and I jumped in the car to head home.

The game went as planned and after our victory we went to the shopping center parking lot on Decker to hang out and celebrate. We weren't hanging long before Adrian linked up with us.

"Look at that star linebacker!"

Adrian comes walking up grinning and laughing.

We mobbed him with fake punches and fist bumps.

I grabbed his hand to shake it again.

1989: A Novella

"Great game big dawg! You tackled errbody"

"Errbody" was Wade's Co-Sign.

Adrian smiled and said, "I had a pretty good game."

Wade said, "Nigga! It was more than pretty good!"

"I'm trying to be humble dawg!" Adrian was mobbed by some females soon after.

I elbowed Wade and said, "See what humble gets you?"

Adrian looked at Wade and told him, "Humble yourself Nigga."

Through a laugh, Wade looks at us and says, "Later for that!"

 We posted up and stood on one of the concrete parking blocks. We had the best time just hanging out and kicking it with our classmates. Soon football season would come to a close and we'd be one step closer to the end of our high school careers. In the meantime, we had a homecoming dance to attend Saturday night. Wade dropped me off at the house and I was in bed before my curfew. I didn't need any problems!

I woke up bright and early to the sound of my Dad cranking up his self-propelled lawn mower. It would only be a matter of time before I heard the familiar rap of his on the window cuing me to get up and do some lawn work...after about 15 minutes the roar of the lawnmower got louder, and closer.

1989: A Novella

RAP PA PAP PAP

That sound meant "Get ya ass up so you can weed eat, edge, and sweep the driveway!". At some point he got tired of saying that, and just used my window pane as the signal for work. I slowly pulled myself together, washed my face and brushed my teeth before heading out to get that yard work done. After the yard work was finished, I cleaned myself up, grabbed a bowl of cereal, and watched Saturday morning cartoons that featured the kids who always learned a valuable lesson by the end of the episode. After that I watched a dance show, and the kung fu movie that followed every Saturday at noon. It was a must to pretend that my voice was overdubbed and fight Rhari while that was going on. Needless to say, he was thoroughly entertained.

After the movie, I called LL and let him know that We were going to leave at 7:30. He was excited to roll with me to the dance.

"I hope they let me in KOT."

"Me too man, If they don't, it won't be because we didn't try."

"See you at 7:30."

My Aunt Beverly dropped off the 300ZX at the house and I couldn't contain my excitement.

"Thank you Auntie!" I threw my arms around her and gave her a big hug.

1989: A Novella

She smiled and said, "You're Welcome Kirven Little, have a good time and be careful."

Before I could say a word, my mama interjected.

"Gull, why are you letting that boy drive that car, when he has nobody's license?"

"He's a good driver, Betty, He'll be fine."

I said, "Mama, I got this."

She shot me a glance and said, "I'm not gonna let you and this heifer worry me!" she shot Aunt Beverly a look before continuing. "If that nigga wreck that car, don't you come over here cryin' and snottin', asking for money to get it fixed, because baby, I ain't got it!"

"Aww Betty..."

"Go on somewhere heifer!"

We all started laughing. My mama was definitely a worrier and I'm sure she wasn't going to truly rest until I got home.

I got dressed and as I prepared to leave, I gave my mama a hug and a kiss on the cheek.

She smiled and called out to me, "Kirven, please be careful in your Auntie's car."

"I will Mama."

"You look very handsome, Kirven...remember..."

1989: A Novella

"I know Mama, don't let nobody touch my weenie or my booty!"

She smiled and started tearing up. She knew that her son was going to his last high school homecoming dance.

LL hopped the fence and met me at the car.

"Oh shit! Is this us, KOT?"

"Hell yeah, it's us. Let's roll!"

We jumped in that little maroon sports car and took off toward Sterling. I put my Big Daddy Kane cassette in the tape deck and all was right with the world. It felt great rolling down Broad and over the tracks while Kane provided the soundtrack for the evening. As much as I wanted to put the car through the paces, I just took it easy and made sure that we arrived at the high school without a scratch on us or more importantly on my Auntie's car.

We walked up to the entrance to the dance like some superstars. It was about to be showtime as LL and I were ready to make our senior homecoming a night to remember. Ms. Christian and Coach Allen were sitting at the table, checking kids in. This was not a development that we had anticipated. Ms. Christian saw me and smiled, I smiled back. Then she saw LL. Her smile evaporated.

"You can't be on school property LL. You have to leave now!"

LL looked crestfallen.

"How did you get here? Kirven, did you bring him?"

1989: A Novella

"Yes ma'am." That was all I could muster in that moment.

Coach Allen sat at the table shaking his head. Normally, he would jump in and give us the business, but it seemed that he might have felt for us a little bit. He stayed on us, but I knew it was because he wanted us to do well and be successful in all aspects of life.

"Kirven, we aren't supposed to let people leave and get back in. Technically, you aren't in yet, so take him home and I will let you in when you return."

"Ms. Christian, can I just walk him in for a minute and then we leave? Please?"

That was my last try. Look sad and hope for the best.

Good assistant principals don't fall for the okey doke.

"Take him home Kirven"

I nodded and we headed out.

As we got back in the car, LL looked at me and said, "Thanks for trying to get me in."

I was focusing on the giant speed bumps in the parking lot.

"We boys, man. We boys. You wanna go back home?"

"Take me over to my Cousin Pete's house."

"Word, you want me to come pick you up?"

"Nah, I'll catch a ride home."

1989: A Novella

We rode in silence up Baker and down Decker. Soon we arrived at Pete's house. LL gave me a fist bump and went inside. I headed back to Sterling and to the dance. All the way back, I thought about how foolish it was to bring LL to the dance when he was suspended from school, yet at the same time, I'd do it again because we looked out for each other.

When I got back to school, once again, Ms. Christian greeted me with a smile. I couldn't really return it. She pulled me to the side and told me that I was a good friend. I smiled a little bit and thanked her. I turned my attention back to the task at hand; there's a party going on.

As I got closer to the commons the music started sounding better and better. The bass was knocking, the high hats were crisp, and the vocals were clear. The DJ had a nice set up. While I was starting to liven up a bit, frustration was still sitting heavy on my chest as I thought about what happened earlier...Ms. Christian's smile disappearing upon our arrival, kept flashing in my mind, like I should've said more... but what? The reality was that there was nothing that I could have done. If anything, I should have tried to stop him from throwing the eggs. I didn't know about that until it happened so there was nothing that I could have done. But now, as I entered The Commons, stepping into the swirling lights and inhaling the aroma from the smoke machine, I was trying to let it go. I made my way around the dance floor making sure I could see and be seen before posting up near the FTP column on the southeast side of The Commons.

1989: A Novella

It wasn't long before I caught up with Wade, Adrian, Kenny, LoLo and the rest of the fellas. They all had their dates and were getting ready to get in the line for pictures.

"Yo Wade, hurry and take your pictures before they start jammin' in here!"

"Word"

I knew that they were only going to play a few rap and R&B songs before the night was over. In the meantime, I was just hanging out and talking to people. I talked to some of my buddies that I had gone to school with since elementary. It was great sharing laughs with them as I didn't get to see them as often because our schedules, while always the same as younger kids, weren't anymore as we pursued our different interests and pursuits.

I was thankful to be something of a teenage sociologist as I got along with many groups at school. This was very helpful at parties as I knew the basics of most genres of music and could dance accordingly. Music videos helped a lot and I learned that as long as I could do a version of the dance that the girl and Bruce Springsteen do in that video where she gets pulled on stage, that I would be okay. So, I spent a lot of time dancing. The Cure, Front 242, and Tears for Fears allowed me the opportunity to show off my "white boy moves" on the dance floor.

Soon the DJ transitioned into some pop hits and I was more in my comfort zone. The sounds of Paula Abdul, New Kids on the Block and Bobby Brown filled The Commons and by this time my friends and their dates were on the dance floor. The party was in full swing. I was actually having a really good time and I thought there was no way that this night could get any better. I was in my element. Dancing and laughing with my friends. Why couldn't life always be like this? Why couldn't everyday end with a dance party?

I got thirsty and walked around for a bit before heading to the restroom and back to the dance floor. I saw the McNair girls and they were not having as much fun as I was.

"What's up y'all?"

Nisha looked disgusted. Twiila frowned. LaShawn sat stoically. Zaunda and Tiffany just sat there with their arms crossed.

Reva looked up and said, "They need to play some rap!"

Rolanda cosigned, "They sholl do because this shit is boring."

They all started nodding and talking as Letitia and Rae Rae went to the DJ to complain.

"I'm sure they got some lined up, they gotta try and make everyone happy." I said as I tried to reassure them that the music was going to include some hip-hop. When they play some, y'all better come dance with me!"

I turned around before I could see their reactions and playfully asked the Lord a favor.

"Lord, please guide the DJs hands and let him play some rap music before the night is done. We don't need the

1989: A Novella

McNair girls having a fit in the homecoming Lord. I ask this in your son Jesus' precious name, amen."

The DJ started playing some slow country music. I groaned.

Walking away, I saw Brittney. She was looking as lovely as ever sitting at a table all by herself.

I approached and said, "Hey, why are you sitting over here by yourself?"

When she looked up, one of the prettiest girls in the school was looking pitiful.

I sat down. "What's wrong Brittney?"

She looked at me with big doe-like brown eyes and said, "Edward's not here."

"Where he at?"

She looked at me and I could tell that she didn't know.

Awkwardly I got up from the table and said, "He'll be here, maybe he's just a little late."

In my mind, I thought that it was totally ridiculous that Edward would not be here on time for a girl like Brittany, especially when you consider that she is not only beautiful, but kind as well. For his sake, I hoped he had a good excuse, because he was never going to hear the end of this.

Meanwhile, I heard the familiar, raspy voice of Tone Loc say, "Let's do it!"

1989: A Novella

I pointed to the heavens and headed toward the dance floor. At this point everyone was on the dance floor as the bass reverberated throughout the building. I made my way through the crowd to find someone to dance with. That someone was my usual school dance partner, Annette.

Annette was tall and slender. She was a cute, creole girl with brown eyes and freckles. She played basketball and ran track. She was a great dancer and I loved dancing with her at parties. I was grooving to the music and was just staring at her, waiting for her to feel like she was being watched…by me. It wasn't long before she noticed. Our eyes met and we both smiled mischievously. Dancing brought us joy, it felt freeing.

We got right down to it. Our chemistry on the dance floor couldn't be denied as we grooved back and forth, to and fro, and move for move. It was like we'd been rehearsing without knowing. Every step, every spin, every hip thrust and gyration were like we were talking through the music, telling a story about what it was like to dance with your musical soulmate. The entire crowd in The Commons started circling up to watch us dance. The crowd was a mass of humanity; thick, loud, drowning in all syncopated funk of the hip hop beats. We opened the circles for others to come in and bust a move. One by one people entered the circle and did their thing in the middle.

Soon Wade got in the middle and started doing his thing. He hit The Cabbage Patch, The Running Man, and The Smurf. He then started to break it down and instinctively I got behind him and kneeled with my right knee forward so he could lean all the way back and bust a move. The crowd started cheering and we went into our kick step routine.

1989: A Novella

After our ending with our customary 360 and the Macka sent the crowd into a frenzy, I went solo, one last time. First, I hit the Reebok and The Prep, with the transitions smooth as frog's hair. Then I started Prepping. Hand and arm movements were sharp and crisp, just to remind everyone how I got down. But for the finale? I had to give them something real, something memorable. I hit The Snake, dropping down low, slithering and twisting till my joints felt like rubber bands, going lower and lower until I had to get face down on the dance floor. I'm sure everyone thought I was going to do the worm, but instead I decided to start vibrating like I was getting electrocuted on the dance floor. The whole place lost their minds. Felt like the roof might lift off. Somehow it didn't!

When I was done, and after all the laughing and high fiving, I stepped off to the side and got something to drink and I attempted to catch my breath against the wall, while watching everything and everyone spin around me. That's when JoAnn, Ronna, and their crew of cheerleaders and homecoming court participants came rushing over, wild-eyed, words tripping over each other.

"Brittany's date didn't show up, Kirven! Edward's not here! He stood her up! She needs somebody to stand with her for the Homecoming court!" JoAnn was beside herself with panic.

Brittany. Yeah, *that* Brittany. Miss Homecoming Queen herself. Looking like a magazine cover and somehow still real. I don't even think I answered. Just nodded. Next thing I knew, they were running into the bathroom to help reapply her makeup and touching up her crown, fixing what didn't even need fixing. She was beautiful and nothing could change that.

I stood, waiting. Trying to find out what my next move was going to be. It wasn't long before I found out.

The lights came up and went low again, grabbing everyone's attention. The DJ grabbed the mic, voice smooth as the track behind him. It was time to introduce the Homecoming court, and there I was, off to the side, waiting to take my place alongside the other court members and their dates.

The crowd was quiet as the DJ announced that the dates could join the members of The Homecoming Court in the middle of the dance floor for a dance. As I walked out to the dance floor, I felt some pats on the back and I got a few high fives as I made my way out to the dance floor.

When I took my place beside Brittany, it hit me—this was one of those rare moments that just made sense. Like I belonged there, like I was meant to stand in that exact spot. It wasn't about votes or titles or who was supposed to be King. For that moment, I simply was. And honestly, nothing else mattered.

The DJ cued up the record and got on the mic one more time.

"Ladies and gentlemen of RSS, please give it up as the homecoming court dances with their dates!"

The crowd started whooping and hollering as they clapped. I took Brittany's hand and led her out to a spot near the RSS seal in the middle of the dance floor.

1989: A Novella

The DJ played a song that would become our prom theme. It was one of those joints that makes you close your eyes while you dance. I held her close, hands light, respectful. One hand on the small of her back and one hand on her waist. Her hair smelled like candy and something else I couldn't name if I tried. We moved slow, small steps, just us and the moment. The Commons got quiet in my mind. Just the two of us left, floating in the middle of it all, holding on to the night.

As we swayed, I started thinking... thinking about senior year, about what might actually be ahead of me and my friends instead of what's just been. I thought about the way things keep trying to break me but somehow, through it all, I'm still here, still standing, still laughing, still dancing.

Maybe... maybe this was the turn.
Maybe all the nonsense wasn't the whole story.
Maybe, after surviving so much, living was still an option.
Maybe... just maybe, living could have meaning and actually be beautiful.

ACKNOWLEDGEMENTS

I feel incredibly blessed to share this work; What a journey it has been to get to this point of sharing such a personal experience!

Chuck D described 1989 the best. It was the most impactful year of my life. The music would form a soundtrack for me that would extend deep into that summer and beyond. Music always has and always will be important to me and always will shape and enhance my experiences. So, I will start these acknowledgements like the liner notes of old:

I want to thank God for the writing ability and the experiences contained in this book. They are real.

Mama (RIP) and Pops, I did it!

The people, places, and events are real. While some of the conversations and events have been embellished for dramatic/comedic effect, it's all based on real and true events.

Special Thanks to Katina for her unwavering support of my vision. I love you. Shout out to Kade for being the best son a man like me could have.

Thanks to my brother Rhari, your feedback let me know that this is exactly the type of project people need to read. Love you brother.

1989: A Novella

Adrian and Jeffrey Wade; y'all been down with me through thick and thin. Thank you for the friendship and the love for over 40 years.

Keith, you said this was my mark on the world; let's see what it do!

A special thanks to Dr. Shalonica Cluse: Your invitation to contribute to the Voices of Black Men project became the catalyst that sparked this project and many more. I am eternally grateful...Thank you.

Thank you to Cindy Griffin for introducing me to my editor, Renita Lofton McKinney.

This wouldn't be possible without help from my editors. Ms. Renita, thank you. Charles Woods, thank you.

For those of you who read chapters, listened to my ideas, and gave me feedback, a sincere thank you.

Heron, Thank you. We just gonna keep throwing each other "The Alley" whenever possible.

Jordyn, I appreciate the feedback. Thank you.

A special thank you to the people that I grew up with. My McNair people, Baytown people, and Barrett Station people. My Harlem, Baytown Jr, and Sterling people. I wish I could name you all one by one...

1989: A Novella

Thank you to my aunts, uncles, and cousins, Auzenne, Barnes, Brooks, Cartwright, Epps, Howard, Jamerson, Reece, Spriggs, and Tillis .

My first friends, Ronnie, Troy and Mario. Much Love to my man A.J. Shout out to Bam Bam.

LoLo you said these stories need to be told. Thank you.

Live and Dynamic. Unified for Self.

Shout out to Snow Belle for the Love and Ninny for the prophecy.

To Kelcy and Megan: Forever connected by 8/8...

Shout out to Prince, Public Enemy, Big Daddy Kane, New Edition, Keith Sweat, Guy, Janet Jackson, Michael Jackson, The Time, Sheila E, The Geto Boys, Royal Flush, Soul II Soul, Sybil, The System, Kid N Play, Ultramagnetic MCs, Special Ed, Kwame', De La Soul, and Slick Rick for providing so much of the soundtrack for my life in 1989.

Last and certainly not least, a huge shout out to the FLAT TOP POSSE. The greatest collective that not enough people know about. What a time we had...WHAT A TIME!

1989: A Novella

ABOUT THE AUTHOR

Kirven Tillis hails from McNair, Texas. For the educator turned consultant, *1989: A Novella* is his foray into writing stories that resonate with the reader. Driven by a passion for both humor and the art of a well-told story, Tillis' work aims to connect with readers on an emotional level, weaving humor into a narrative that lingers long after the final page.

Made in the USA
Columbia, SC
23 July 2025

504b4be5-d58b-4289-994f-28d355466167R01